Loyalty Unplugged

Loyalty Unplugged

The plain truth about building customer loyalty and boosting revenues profitably.

Dennis L. Duffy

Loyalty Rules, Inc.

www.loyalty-rules.com

ISBN 1-59196-030-4

To
Nancy

Contents

Chapter One

Unplugged

I have spent more than a dozen years working with companies to develop and manage customer loyalty programs. Two things are clear to me. First, companies have an appetite for guidelines on developing customer loyalty. Second, developing customer loyalty is one of the single most powerful ways to enhance a brand and create shareholder value.

I've seen too many people over complicate the concept of customer loyalty. I decided to demystify the concept in this book and remove all the complications. I set out to tell the plain truth about customer loyalty: what it means and how to develop it. That's why I've called this book *Loyalty Unplugged*.

I use the word loyalty to describe the essential principle this book will explore and demystify. I use loyalty to describe the feeling customers have toward a brand. It is the feeling that compels customers to turn left instead of right to visit a particular retail brand. It's the feeling that causes customers to think twice before accepting a competitive offer to switch to a competing Internet access service. It's the feeling that makes customers come back and test drive one new model vehicle over another.

Regardless of the industry you're in, loyalty is the tiebreaker that makes customers think twice about another brand. Loyalty creates a reluctance to defect among customers. Ultimately, loyalty delivers enormous economic value to your brand by increasing the lifetime value of customers.

I discuss loyalty at two levels: loyalty strategy and loyalty tactics. Loyalty strategy involves getting your company right for customers. It's the equivalent of getting your house in order. It's ensuring that your product and value proposition, your service and your communication channels are conducive to developing loyalty. It also involves assessing your culture as a company to ensure it creates an appropriate platform for developing loyalty. Loyalty tactics are the integrated marketing efforts that actively engage your customers in a dialogue and often deploy exclusive benefits and rewards that keep your best customers alert and attentive to your brand.

In a nutshell, loyalty strategy involves getting your company in shape to keep customers and loyalty tactics are the proactive efforts to increase customer value through relationships and special benefits. It's important to keep the two levels of the loyalty discussion clear. Loyalty strategy becomes the platform, loyalty tactics become the active extension to key customer segments.

There are many other terms used to describe loyalty. While many other authors and speakers will split hairs about the differences, I'll be a lightning rod for controversy and declare that all these concepts are simply enablers for customer loyalty. Each concept is a means to an end. The end is loyalty.

Customer Relationship Management (CRM)

Customer Relationship Management (CRM) is an important enabling concept. It represents the principle of creating a comprehensive view of the organization and its methods of collecting, consolidating and using customer information. The aim of CRM is to be more intelligent about how to communicate with customers, how to prioritize customers within your customer service organization and how to create value propositions and offers that are more relevant to each customer.

Simply put, CRM involves the construction of an information architecture that allows the organization to become a customer-centric learning machine. But it is a means to an end. It requires a loyalty strategy to actually leverage the infrastructure to create business results by increasing customer value.

Don't get me wrong, CRM is important. But in my mind, CRM is a subset of loyalty strategy. It's the infrastructure and information systems component of getting your company ready to keep customers.

Enterprise Relationship Management (ERM)

This is what I call the big brother of CRM. While CRM often looks at one channel or one division, ERM involves a comprehensive (and mammoth) review of the entire organization. ERM also takes it a step further and examines the organizational structure, roles and responsibilities in executing loyalty activities.

Electronic Customer Relationship Management (eCRM)

Whew! Another one. This is the on-line version of CRM. It's CRM on the Internet.

Relationship Marketing

A somewhat dated term, this describes the process of cultivating customer relationships by deploying targeted and relevant communication (by traditional mail or e-mail). This is a means to an end. The objective of Relationship Marketing is to create loyalty.

Relationship Management

The earlier term for CRM.

One to One Marketing

This is an important concept and one that propelled many marketers into action. It is the theoretical concept of communication with each customer as if you were communicating solely with that customer. This is a concept and a means to an end. The end it seeks to create is loyalty.

Frequency Marketing

This concept originated in the travel business and originally focused on frequency of transaction. It has been expanded to parallel loyalty but still gets misunderstood because of the literal interpretation.

Focus on Loyalty

Now that we have many of the related terms clarified, let's discuss the loyalty concept itself. Simply put, loyalty is about improving retention and increasing share of customer. It's about keeping customers longer than you otherwise would. It's about getting a greater share of a customer's business than you otherwise would. It's that simple. It's that complicated.

I've heard many statements about the concept of loyalty. Here are some of the concepts and my perspectives.

"Loyalty is Dead" ... "There is no Such Thing as Loyalty"

I think these people are taking it too literally. We're not talking about German Shepherds lying at our feet. We're talking about customers. We're trying to create the difference between retention and defection. Dog-like loyalty to a brand will rarely happen. But we're not talking about the tireless and unconditional loyalty that a dog exhibits toward its master. We just want to influence customer behavior in subtle and effective ways to increase the likelihood they'll stick with our brand.

"You Can't Buy Loyalty"

True. But this statement actually has a relationship with the one above. We're not trying to create a tireless dog-like loyalty. We're trying to create a reluctance to defect and a tendency to stick with our brand. While we cannot buy this, we must spend money to earn it. We'll spend our money several ways. We'll spend our money implementing loyalty strategy and we'll spend our money executing loyalty programs. The investment – well planned – will create the equivalent (in terms of customer behavior) of loyalty.

The loyalty pursuit allegedly started with airline frequent traveler programs. In fact, the pursuit of loyalty began much earlier. Remember collecting Green Stamps? Box tops? Simple but effective ways to get customers to think about your brand and stick with it. Welcome to loyalty.

The development of loyalty is a big thing. It requires high level commitment –- from the top down. It requires a vision and the appropriate culture to support that vision. It's a way of doing business. It can be an incredibly rewarding way of doing business, but for some companies it's a big shift. It's a big shift toward managing customers instead of managing products. It's in everything you do.

You're about to take a journey. A journey to build customer loyalty. The journey will create a framework and a set of guidelines for developing loyalty in your business. The journey will illustrate loyalty in action with examples from dozens of companies.

Don't turn back. You'll enjoy the trip.

Chapter Two

Benefits of Loyalty

The benefits of customer loyalty are all economic in the long run. Some are easier to quantify than others, but if you take a long term, customer lifetime value approach to looking at your business, all can be quantified.

Lifetime Value

Let's take a look at lifetime value. For the sake of this section let's use a very simple example. Assume that Duffy's Depot is a retail establishment. The average customer of Duffy's Depot buys $1,000 in goods each year at an average gross margin of 35%. Furthermore, the average customer stays with Duffy's Depot for five years (I know this is oversimplified for you lifetime value fanatics, but bear with me or skip over this example – this is just to ensure everyone gets off on the right foot).

The lifetime value calculation involves discounting each of the future profit streams to present value. It is a simple net present value calculation that most of us have experienced at some point in our education or careers. If I use a 10% discount rate for my calculation, the numbers look like this:

Lifetime Value Example

Year	Gross Profit	Discount Factor	Present Value
One	$ 350.00	1.1000	$ 318.18
Two	$ 350.00	1.2100	$ 289.26
Three	$ 350.00	1.3310	$ 262.96
Four	$ 350.00	1.4641	$ 239.05
Five	$ 350.00	1.6105	$ 217.32
Total			$ 1,326.78

Now, imagine you're able to improve the retention rate and keep customers for six years, rather than just five.

The lifetime value improves as follows:

Lifetime Value Example

Year	Gross Profit	Discount Factor	Present Value
One	$ 350.00	1.1000	$ 318.18
Two	$ 350.00	1.2100	$ 289.26
Three	$ 350.00	1.3310	$ 262.96
Four	$ 350.00	1.4641	$ 239.05
Five	$ 350.00	1.6105	$ 217.32
Six	$ 350.00	1.7716	$ 197.57
Total			$ 1,524.34

As you can see, the lifetime value has increased $197.56 – a 15% improvement. If you're also able to get a greater share of the customer's business, the lifetime value improvement is even better.

Let's assume that the average sales increase is 15%. The new lifetime value, considering an improvement in retention and in share of customer is as follows:

Lifetime Value Example

Year	Gross Profit	Discount Factor	Present Value
One	$ 402.50	1.1000	$ 365.91
Two	$ 402.50	1.2100	$ 332.64
Three	$ 402.50	1.3310	$ 302.40
Four	$ 402.50	1.4641	$ 274.91
Five	$ 402.50	1.6105	$ 249.92
Six	$ 402.50	1.7716	$ 227.20
Total			$ 1,752.99

The lifetime value has been increased by another $228.65. The combined impact of both improvements is $426.21 – a total increase of 28% over the original lifetime value of $1,524.34.

That covers the impact of improvements in retention and share of customer. Many people fail to look beyond that, but there are some extremely powerful benefits associated with customer loyalty that go beyond the obvious.

Cost Savings

Customers who frequently shop Duffy's Depot over a period of time get to know what Duffy's Depot is all about and the merchandise that's available in the store. They require less assistance because they are so familiar with the brand. In some cases loyal customers know more about your brand than some of your employees do. A loyalty customer's questions are more relevant and to the point. They come to the store with a fairly clear vision of what is available at Duffy's Depot and what it takes to shop at Duffy's Depot. As a result, these customers are more efficient in terms of the way they use Duffy's Depot resources to conduct transactions. This is an important ancillary benefit to customer loyalty that is often overlooked.

Referrals

Customers who become familiar with Duffy's Depot and its merchandise mention it to their friends and acquaintances. People like to feel smart and "in the know." They like to have an opinion. Loyalty customers won't hesitate to make recommendations to friends and neighbors.

Complain Rather Than Defect

This is a subtle one, but it is a benefit I believe in from experiences with a variety of retail marketers. Customers who are loyal and who are a part of a well-executed customer loyalty program feel like they are stakeholders in the retail brand. When they have a bad experience they complain. They make a phone call, they ask for the manager or they do something else to make sure their issue is addressed. They believe in the brand. They feel that it's their brand. They want to fix it. They complain rather than quietly defecting. This "second chance" opportunity is very important in today's business environment in which customers are so fickle.

Channel Migration

Loyal customers are more likely to buy through alternative channels. I'm talking principally about the Internet. Most retailers today sell through traditional channels (bricks and mortar stores, maybe a catalog) and on-line. Loyal customers who are familiar with your brand are much more likely to buy through multiple channels, increasing their total consumption and reducing your cost of doing business with them.

Many companies fear that channel migration represents cannibalization. I've seen an example of a traditional bricks and mortar retailer that had only a 10% overlap between their on-line and off-line customers. I've also seen examples that suggest multi-channel shoppers buy more (in total, across all channels) than single channel shoppers. This suggests that providing many ways for customers to buy your products may increase customer value.

Loyalty is about managing customers not products. It's also about making customers more important than channels. In too many companies today there is an inordinate amount of time spent haggling about channel turf and product turf and inadequate time spent haggling about customers.

Unaided Awareness

Loyal customers are much more likely to have your brand top of mind in your category. This manifests itself in terms of an increase in share of customer and an improvement in retention. But it also helps with referrals and it helps with "bring alongs" in which loyal customers actually bring other customers (friends, relatives) to your brand. The combined impact of unaided awareness improvements shows up in many places. I have seen dramatic improvements in unaided awareness due to customer loyalty strategies.

Greater Awareness of Brand Assets

Loyal customers tend to be more aware of some of the auxiliary benefits your brand offers. It has been demonstrated that greater awareness of auxiliary benefits, or "hidden assets," has an impact on retention and share of customer. For instance, a retailer I worked with found that loyal customers were more familiar with their free delivery service. This familiarity led to greater sales as a result of taking advantage of the free delivery. A telecommunications company found that loyal customers were more aware of the services provided by their dedicated relationship managers. These customers tended to stay with the brand longer because they felt they received better value. The perception of better value was a function of understanding the services offered by the relationship managers and taking advantage of those services.

Turn Left Rather Than Turn Right

I use this to describe the subtle impact of a loyalty strategy. At times, a brand choice is made at the last minute. Do I turn left or turn right? Do I shop Lowe's or Home Depot? Is it Barnes & Noble or Borders? Is it Amazon.com or BN.com? The subtle, psychological reluctance to defect created by a loyalty strategy often makes the difference.

As you can see, there are some tremendous benefits associated with customer loyalty. Many are inter-related and virtually all can be quantified and measured. But you can also see that a loyalty strategy is genuinely that – a strategy. It's in everything you do and it can have an amazing positive impact on your brand.

Chapter Three

The Loyalty Landscape

Let's take a look at loyalty-building strategies and tactics in some real companies.

Much of the foundation of loyalty marketing is linked to the travel industry. In fact many companies are tempted to mimic frequent flier programs. I won't spend too much time on travel programs, but I will point out how different the travel industry is from most others.

Travel Industry

We all get excited about frequent traveler programs. Whether it's frequent flier or frequent guest, anyone who travels regularly is in the game. The perks and rewards are impressive. Upgrades to first class make our mundane business travel more tolerable. Free business class tickets to another continent make a much-needed vacation more enjoyable. Seven days and six nights at a top-notch golf resort. What's not to like?

Business travelers control very large relationships between their business and an airline or hotel company. Frequent fliers have the power to redirect large quantities of spending toward the airline of their choice. Some may spend $20,000 or more each year on airline tickets. Where else does a single consumer control so much spending? There aren't too many situations that are this dramatic and that's one of the reasons the travel industry is so different from most others.

High fixed and low variable costs. Airlines and hotels have a substantial investment in infrastructure and, within a relevant range, the variable cost of delivering an incremental unit of product is insignificant. When an airline sells one more seat on a flight, the incremental profit percentage is substantial.

Idle capacity. The cost of "giving away" free product is small because of the high fixed and low variable cost structure. One can make the argument that free flights and free phone usage displace paid consumption and represent an opportunity cost or an example of cannibalization. Without doubt there is some displacement of revenue, but the impact of improved retention and increased share of customer more than offsets the displacement.

Difference between perceived value and actual cost. When you earn a free ticket the perceived value to you is enormous. Most people don't waste their free trips on cheap ones. We go far and we go first class. But because of the nature of the industry, the actual cost is low to the travel company. There is virtually no other industry in which there is such a disparity between the actual cost of free product and its perceived value through the eyes of the customer.

Outside the Travel Industry

Some non-travel companies build links to the travel industry. Some hope to "bottle the magic" of free travel. Others use the travel link to leverage the passion frequent travelers have for miles and points. Once you're playing the game, earning a little extra for things like your long distance telephone service can be compelling.

MCI Worldcom

MCI Worldcom is one of the leading telecommunications companies in the United States. They run a program called MCI Worldcom Frequent Flyer Rewards. It allows customers to earn miles on the airline of their choice simply for having MCI as their long distance carrier.

Long distance telephone service is a low-involvement decision. Let's face it. We're not all sitting at home agonizing over who we want as a long distance company. We want our phone to work and we want the best price. Beyond that, we don't really care who our long distance carrier is. We need a reason to choose one over another.

MCI Worldcom Frequent Flyer Rewards does that for a certain segment of the population. It's the segment that is already playing the frequent flyer game and wants another way to add some miles to their accounts. This program isn't going to get the non-frequent traveler earning enough miles to take many trips. But it will enhance the earning rate for someone who is a frequent traveler. This program becomes the tie breaker. It becomes the reason for a frequent traveler to pick MCI Worldcom over the competition.

Members of Frequent Flyer Rewards earn five miles for every dollar spent. Members also get a 3,000 mile bonus for enrolling in this program. The miles can be applied to many airline frequent flyer programs, including American Airlines, America West, China Airlines, Delta, Hawaiian Airlines, Korean Air, Midwest Express, Southwest Airlines, United Airlines and US Airways. (Note that the structure of the deal is different for Southwest Airlines because the structure of their frequent flyer program is a bit different from the rest).

Members pay a $3.95 monthly fee to participate in this program. That's an inconsequential fee to frequent travelers who are willing to fork over a few bucks per month to accelerate their earning pace to get more upgrades and free trips.

MCI Worldcom is smart enough to know that Frequent Flyer Rewards isn't for everyone. So they have another program. It's called Blockbuster Free Flix.

Free Flix allows members to earn one free video rental for every $25 spent per month on MCI Worldcom long distance. The free video rental may be used for a VHS tape, a DVD or a video game. Members get six free rentals for signing up.

This program appeals to the mainstream population. The average household can earn a free video or two each month just for using their phone. It's enough of a tie-breaker to make the average family think about one long-distance carrier over another. This is also a high utility reward. Most households can relate to a free video and they understand what it's worth.

Blockbuster Video

Blockbuster Video is the category leader in video rental in the United States. The company has its own program that gives customers a reason to consolidate all their video rental business. It's called Blockbuster Rewards. It's a fee-based program in which customers pay $9.95 per year to participate. The primary hook in this program is the ability to earn a free video rental for every five paid video rentals in a month.

This is a smart program for two reasons. First, the earning structure. Members earn a free rental for five paid rentals in a month. If members don't reach five in a month, the counter resets to zero going into the following month. This helps Blockbuster avoid the classic dilemma of rewarding ordinary behavior. Because the reward is skewed toward heavier rental activity it is more likely to be rewarding incremental behavior. Because the counter is reset each month, Blockbuster isn't carrying an increasingly larger liability.

The second smart element is the fee. The fee is a filter. It ensures that the people joining this program are serious. Blockbuster doesn't get a lot of frivolous members. Customers who join are now engaged with Blockbuster. They'll think twice before renting around because they've made a monetary commitment to Blockbuster. As a result, Blockbuster gets a greater share of the average member's business.

There are other benefits associated with Blockbuster Rewards. Members get a free "favorite" (a non-new release) each month. Members also have the opportunity to get a free favorite with a paid rental on certain days of the week. There's also a newsletter members receive monthly that talks up new releases. It's a good value proposition that focuses on incremental business by increasing share of customer.

Barnes & Noble

A major player in the bookstore category, Barnes & Noble launched its Readers' Advantage program to do just what Blockbuster did in the video business: consolidate share of customer.

Barnes & Noble commands a $25 annual fee for this program. In exchange for that fee, members get a 10% discount at point of sale at bricks and mortar stores. Members also get five percent off at BN.COM. Readers' Advantage serves up a high quality communication vehicle in the form of a free subscription to *Book Magazine* and members have access to www.readersadvantage.com for exclusive author interviews and essays. Barnes & Noble invites members to exclusive literary events at local stores.

Readers' Advantage is a high quality program. It's well promoted and tastefully delivered at point of sale. The associates in Barnes & Noble stores do a nice job of explaining the program to customers. The $25 fee is hefty. I'm sure a lot of customers do the math quickly in their head to determine whether or not they'll spend $250 in a year to get enough of a discount to pay back the fee. Once paid, I'm sure the fee makes customers think twice about shopping other bookstores and, as a result, they consolidate as much of their spending as possible at Barnes & Noble.

Waldenbooks

Waldenbooks is another major player in the mall-based bookstore category. Their Preferred Reader program has been around for years. It's another fee-based program.

Customers pay $10 per year to become members. Members receive 10% off most purchases (magazines, newspapers and gift certificates are excluded). Members also earn points in this program at a rate of one point per dollar spent. Once a member earns 100 points, a reward certificate is issued that gives the member an additional five dollars (above and beyond the 10% point of sale discount). The effective benefit rate in this program is 15% when you combine the discount and the points.

There is also a Preferred Reader co-branded Visa credit card. The Visa allows members to earn additional Preferred Reader points for spending anywhere. Members earn one point for every five dollars spent on the card anywhere. The rate is much higher (one point per dollar spent) when the card is used at Waldenbooks, Brentano's Bookstores and Walden-By-Mail.

Preferred Reader is another good program for getting
customers to consolidate their business with a single brand.
Once you pay the fee you're committed.

McDonald's

Everyone knows McDonald's. In the intensely competitive
quick service restaurant category, McDonald's is one of the
leaders. However, the fight for loyalty among fickle
consumers is a tough one. McDonald's recently tested a
program called Road2Rewards.

Road2Rewards was focused on McDonald's younger
customers. The imagery in this program featured teens on
skateboards. The program awarded points for McDonald's
purchases. The points in the program were redeemable for
McDonald's Extra Value Meals, free movie tickets and free
music CDs.

Here's how the program worked. Customers received
special coupons that were printed at point of sale with
every transaction. Each coupon had a unique 15-digit code
number on it and instructions for logging in at
www.road2rewards.com. Customers registered and posted
their coupon codes on-line. Points were awarded based on
the dollar amount of the transaction. Once members earned
enough points to redeem, they requested one of the three
different reward options. The program was administered
entirely on-line. All customer communication (with the
exception of the coupons and point of sale promotional
elements) was done via e-mail.

This program is interesting for several reasons. First, it demonstrates that some programs can be administered and tracked without issuing member cards or key chain tags. Customers receive certificates and then may enroll in the program after the fact and still get credit for past transactions. Second, it is administered entirely on-line and communicated completely via e-mail. It proves that off-line programs can be managed relatively inexpensively using on-line thinking.

This program ran for a short period in a test market. As of this writing, I think McDonald's is contemplating doing it again. This time perhaps longer.

Evian

This bottled water brand ran a limited-time program called Upgrade to Evian. It was an interesting move for a consumer packaged goods brand, reaching out directly to consumers.

The program was promoted on the water bottle labels. Each label had a unique code number on it (on the inside of the label, only accessible by peeling the label from the bottle). The lure to get customers to join was a game of chance. Some lucky member would win the use of a private jet for a vacation. Not bad.

Customers joined at www.evian.com and became members. Members posted their code numbers and earned points. Members also got an entry in the game of chance for every code entered. Points were redeemable for Evian merchandise (watches, T-shirts and hats).

This program is intriguing because it's a package goods
company developing a direct relationship with the
consumer. Packaged goods companies more typically have
a relationship with the retailer who has a direct relationship
with the consumer. This program is another example of
successfully executing a program for an off-line brand,
using on-line thinking. It's also a fine example of using a
game of chance with an alluring grand prize to get
consumers to engage in a program that doesn't necessarily
offer the most compelling earned prizes. In the end, Evian
gets a few steps closer to understanding exactly who their
customers are and how much they buy.

Wells Fargo

Wells Fargo is the fifth-largest bank in the United States (at
the time of this writing). They offer customers a choice
when it comes to loyalty programs tied to their credit card
products. The programs are similar in structure, but they
vary in terms of the feel of the rewards and the annual fee.

Wells Fargo Rewards carries a $19 annual fee. Prime
Rewards is aimed at a more upscale audience and carries a
$70 annual fee. Both are points-based programs. Members
earn points based on their purchase activity. Both
programs offer a variety of retail-oriented and travel-
oriented rewards. Some of the redemption options include
shopping with retailers such as Macy's, Dillards, The
Sharper Image, The Right Start, Gap, Old Navy and
Toys R Us. Prime Rewards adds some upscale redemption
options that include brands like Saks Fifth Avenue and
Ritz-Carlton.

The programs that Wells Fargo offers are not breakthroughs. They do, however, represent choice for Wells Fargo customers. Many banking programs are fairly static in their offering. These offer customers a bit of flexibility.

Bank of America

Typically the term "loyalty program" instantly conjures up images of points earned and redeemed for some kind of "free stuff." But there are more ways to earn loyalty.

Bank of America demonstrates its understanding of loyalty with its Advantage Checking product. This product has a bundle of special benefits aimed at keeping customers.

Checking accounts are low involvement products. Once you've chosen a bank for your checking account relationship, you typically stay with that bank unless you move or have a bad experience that motivates you to terminate the relationship. Sometimes a few extra benefits are enough to get customers to stick with one checking accounting instead of switching to another.

The benefits of Advantage Checking include things such as:

- Free checks and checkbook cover
- Rate bonus on certificates of deposit
- Preferred rates on money market accounts, loans and credit lines
- No-fee platinum check card
- No-fee travelers checks
- Free safe deposit box
- Free stop payments
- No-fee cashier's checks
- No-fee money orders

Bank of America also offers some products to lure the frequent traveler. They issue credit and debit cards linked with the US Airways Dividend Miles frequent flyer program. This helps Bank of America get as large a share as possible of its frequent traveler customer base.

The Platinum Visa Card with Rewards helps small companies make the most of their spending. Member companies earn points based on the usage of multiple credit cards all issued under an umbrella account. The points are redeemable for merchandise and gift certificates that the company can use. The program also offers additional benefits such as a personal concierge service, extended warranty program, travel accident insurance and auto rental insurance. This is a good bundle of benefits and provides companies with a reason to choose one credit card program over another.

Bank Champaign

Not exactly a household name. This is a local bank in Champaign, Illinois. I've included it here because it's a good example of the little guy trying hard to compete with big banks.

Bank Champaign offers a checking account that awards miles in the American Airlines AAdvantage program. There is no fee with this program as long is there is an average daily balance of $1,000 in the account (if not, the fee is seven dollars per month). Miles are awarded monthly on the following schedule of average daily balance in the account:

- Daily balance of $500 earns 250 miles.
- Daily balance of $1,000 earns 250 miles.
- Daily balance of $2,000 earns 500 miles.
- Daily balance of $3,000 earns 750 miles.
- Daily balance of $4,000 earns 1,000 miles.
- Daily balance of $5,000 earns 1,250 miles.

This is a great program aimed at giving customers a reason to stay with Bank Champaign. It's another example of what it takes to get customers to think twice about a low involvement decision. A fine tie breaker.

Bank of Asia

This is a bank in Thailand with one of the most comprehensive loyalty offerings I've seen. They have managed to tie together many different product lines to create a compelling reason for customers to consolidate all of their financial services business with Bank of Asia.

Customers earn points on the following:

- Spending on Asia Visa card
- Balance in savings account
- Use of Asia Visa Electron Debit card
- Payments on housing loans, with a bonus for consistent on-time payments
- Use of personal credit line
- Use of Bank of Asia's ATMs at least once per month
- Use of Western Union Money Transfer

This kind of program is often difficult for a bank to execute because of the many internal silos of product management. Clearly Bank of Asia has learned to manage customers instead of products. Its integrated loyalty program demonstrates this.

Imation

Imation is a supplier of data management equipment, and graphic arts and color reproduction equipment and services. Imation products are sold through retailers and catalogs.

The Rewards Imation Program (RIP) offers members (consumers and businesses) points for purchases of Imation products. Imation has specially labeled products that include a unique authentication code. Customers register for RIP at rip.imation.com. Once they've registered, they input UPCs and authentication codes for the products they purchase. Points accumulate in the account and members may redeem for a variety of merchandise such as CDs, DVDs and software.

This is another example of a program administered and promoted on-line. It's also an example of a brand that doesn't usually interact directly with the customer. Just like Evian, Imation is reaching out directly and building a relationship with the customer it doesn't typically get to know.

Single Brand versus Coalition Programs

The programs I've described so far are single brand programs. These programs are sponsored by a single brand that is clearly the star. Single brand programs are often powerful tools for building customer loyalty. But they require a commitment and an investment.

Coalition programs exist simply to be programs. There is no star brand. The program itself is the star brand. Multiple partners team up in coalition programs to create a larger value proposition.

One such coalition program is uPromise.

uPromise

A great value proposition. Consumers join uPromise and earn credits toward children's future college education.

A compelling offer indeed. A coalition program must have an offer that really makes consumers want to play the game. Many young parents are interested in getting started early when it comes to planning for a child's college education. Many grandparents are interested in helping offset the cost of their grandchildren's education by doing whatever they can.

uPromise allows everyone to help. Consumers enroll at www.upromise.com. Consumers earn credits from dozens of partners. The earning process is made relatively easy by allowing members to register multiple credit cards with uPromise. When a registered credit card is used with a uPromise partner, the member automatically earns. No special cards to carry. No membership numbers to memorize. Offset your college costs by doing what you've always done.

The partner list is compelling. McDonald's is a partner. AT&T is a partner (their alternative to MCI Worldcom's Blockbuster Free Flix). ExxonMobil. Coca-Cola. General Motors. Toys R Us. Plenty of partners that give uPromise members ways to earn credits every day.

Expanding the Loyalty Landscape

I've offered a variety of loyalty examples covering consumer brands and business-to-business brands. For more examples, visit the Loyalty Library at our website www.loyalty-rules.com.

There are literally thousands of loyalty programs running right now around the world. These programs range from punch card programs at the local dry cleaner to massive coalition programs linking huge global brands. And there are more on the way.

But before you leap into loyalty in your company, stop and think. Consider what you're setting out to do. Consider the current state of your company and how "customer friendly" you really are. Now that I've whetted your appetite, let's take a closer look at what it means to get your house in order.

Chapter Four

Getting Your House In Order

"I just work here."

That's the response I get from front line associates in companies that don't have their house in order. These are companies that haven't recognized how important customers are. I have recently experienced the "I just work here" comment with my cable TV provider. I was calling to add an extra service. While reviewing my account, this poor agent learned from his supervisor that my current service hadn't been priced right to begin with. They weren't charging me enough.

I explained that it didn't seem to make sense. They set the price. Their pricing is sufficiently confusing anyway so it's virtually impossible for the average customer like me to figure it out. In fact it's so confusing their own people can't interpret it.

This guy had been told by his supervisor to set me straight about the pricing, and increase my base monthly fee even if I didn't buy the new service. He was also told to explain to me that I was lucky they weren't going to charge me retroactively for all the months I was getting away with a deal.

Companies that don't have their house in order treat customers as adversaries. They often feel that customers are trying to lie, cheat and steal their way through life by getting a better deal from everyone they do business with. These companies don't promote an atmosphere of listening and collaboration. Instead they promote an atmosphere of suspicion and closed-mindedness.

Does Your Company Allow Customers to be Loyal?

I often ask this question. Does your company allow customers to be loyal? Does your culture encourage and support customer collaboration? Much of this has to do with the extent to which employees in your company are allowed to make decisions to take care of customers.

There are legendary stories of exceptional customer service. The retail employee that allowed a customer to return a set of tires even though the retailer didn't sell tires. The hotel employee who jumped on a plane to ensure a guest had his laptop computer in time for an important presentation. These examples demonstrate a common thread in the two companies. Employees are encouraged and allowed to make decisions to help customers. Even if the decisions cost the company money.

Let me point out a psychological barrier that many companies face. This is a barrier that keeps many companies from establishing the kind of environment that allows this level of customer collaboration. It's a barrier of fear and mistrust.

Management in some companies fear that allowing employees to make decisions may cost the company too much money. Fear is linked to mistrust. Management does not trust employees to make rational decisions. In fact, employees typically make extremely rational decisions. When they're allowed to make choices, they agonize over these choices to be sure they make sense. On balance, employees want to do what's right. Given the duty, responsibility and authority to make things right by customers, they will exercise their judgement as if the money were their own.

Culture

Is your company's culture one that focuses on customers? Culture is created and sustained by the words and action of its leaders. Do the leaders in your company talk about customers in an open and honest way? Do leaders encourage employees to think about customers when they make daily decisions?

You can typically get a sense of an organization's culture by sitting through a few meetings. I've been in meetings in which people don't want to debate with a higher ranking person in their organization. People are careful about what they say. These are signs of an organization that practices management by fear. People are afraid they'll get punished for doing or saying the wrong thing. Choices are carefully

considered. Risks are not taken. Everything is safe.
Innovation is non-existent.

I've been in meetings in which everyone engages, speaks
their mind and debates. Regardless of rank, everyone
jumps in and has their say. This is an organization that
genuinely encourages thinking, innovation, ideas and
choices. This is an organization that is likely more tuned-in
to its customers as well. This organization learns from its
mistakes. It innovates. It's not afraid to be different. It has
passion.

Managing Customers

Manage customers, not just products and channels.

There are many organizational silos that preclude
companies from achieving breakthroughs in marketing.
Bank of Asia was able to innovate and implement a loyalty
strategy that touched all its product lines. It's not
something you see in most banks. Barnes & Noble was
able to bridge the gap between channels to ensure its
Readers' Advantage program spans bricks and mortar
stores as well as its on-line business.

I'm not suggesting that companies abandon the idea of
establishing accountability for a product line or a channel
of distribution. I'm saying there must be an element of the
organization that has responsibility for customers. There
must be responsibility and authority for ensuring that
marketing strategies and programs make sense through the
eyes of the customer. This role is the customer advocate.

Marketing and IT

Some of the best ideas ever conceived never happened because of barriers between the marketing department and the information technology (IT) department. Is this an issue in your company?

Some of it comes down to a language barrier. Marketing people often get frustrated because they feel they can't get a straight answer from their IT counterparts. IT people often get frustrated because they feel their marketing counterparts don't know what they're doing, or they don't understand the complexity of what they're proposing.

You've got to understand the source of this language barrier. IT can, at times, be a thankless job. Often blamed, rarely commended. That's their tagline. Something's broke, they hear about it for sure. Something's working perfectly, not a word. These kinds of situations can create environments in which IT departments don't want to innovate. They simply want to do what they must and avoid making mistakes.

Keep in mind this is not because they're bad people. They just need to be made a part of the process early on. Create a cross-functional team and include your IT counterparts in all your discussions about loyalty. Don't just bring them in when you need to talk about a specific thing you want them to do. That kind of behavior makes people feel like vendors, not partners.

Disparate Customer Information

Does your company have loads of customer information
trapped in multiple, incompatible and inaccessible systems?
Not unusual. If you don't, congratulations. You're one of
the lucky ones. If you do, don't fret. You're not alone.
This dilemma is a typical one that companies must
overcome to get their house in order. Unfortunately, the
initiative is often over-engineered. The requirements
discussion takes years. The specifications won't fit in a
single binder. It never gets off the ground.

The key to success in bringing together multiple, disparate
data sources is focus and pragmatism. Your organization
needs to see that it can be done. Focus on short-term
milestones you can deliver on. These milestones create
enthusiasm and momentum in your company and help keep
your efforts alive.

Depending on the type of company you're in, you may
already have customer transaction level information. If you
don't, there's another barrier to overcome.

Does your technology support the linkage between a
customer number and transaction information? Never mind
for the time being how you'll get the customer to identify
himself. That's another story. If he does identify himself,
can you capture that ID number and link it with his
transactions. If you can't now, what will it take to be able
to do it? This is another big marketing/IT collaboration
question.

What to do Next

Don't feel paralyzed if you're house is not in order.
Getting your house in order is a journey, not a destination.
You'll always be working on it.

I encourage people to identify the most critical things that
need to be addressed before undertaking a loyalty initiative.
It doesn't mean you need to fix everything. In fact, it's
better to test some simple, loyalty building marketing
activities while you correct some of your organizational
deficiencies. Creating and sharing marketing success
stories will help you build enthusiasm for more
organizational improvements.

Break your problems into manageable chunks and move
forward. Once you've considered the extent to which
you're house is in order, it's time to move on to the
Customer Loyalty Audit.

Chapter Five

The Customer Loyalty Audit

In the previous chapter we talked about getting your house in order. Now we're going to review what you need to do to surround yourself with the right information to make informed decisions about the best tactical approach to loyalty.

Stop. I know what you're about to do. You're going to delegate this. Forget about it. The best leaders open their eyes to the real situation in their company. They accept the good, the bad and the ugly. They also accept the fact that some things can only be fixed by top management. If you don't get involved, this will never get off the ground. You can't send someone else to be your eyes. Lead this process yourself. Use your eyes.

The Customer Loyalty Audit (or CLA) is a comprehensive review of your situation with an eye toward determining your options. It also helps identify inconsistencies, inefficiencies and potential obstacles that should be corrected and overcome as you move forward with your loyalty efforts. The CLA (much like any other review process) cannot answer your questions or fix your problems. You must answer your questions. You must fix your problems. The CLA provides a framework for organizing information and for identifying tasks.

The CLA is organized into five major sections:

1. The Customer
2. The Competition
3. The Communication
4. The Operation
5. The Technology

Each section of the CLA outlines basic questions and provides commentary and guidance for helping you weave your way through each section in your own organization.

Think about the process of going through the CLA like the process of taking a test. The SAT. The GMAT. You get the idea. The key is this: don't spend too much time getting hung up on one question. Come back to it. The intent of the CLA is to get through the process in a matter of four to ten weeks. If you spend too much time trying to get perfect answers and perfect information you'll never make progress. Move swiftly. Use information, insight, intuition and common sense. Chances are that's what got you to where you are today. Trust it.

Here's how to work with the CLA process. Make lists of all the potential answers to the questions in each section. There are typically no right and wrong answers. These are not black and white questions. Each of the answers addresses a portion of the question. Make your own list of potential answers and gather lists by interviewing others in your organization. Consolidate the lists and highlight the answers that may be addressable in a loyalty program.

For instance, "convenience" will certainly appear under the question, "Why don't customers give us all their business?" We can't do much about convenience within the scope of loyalty. Don't get me wrong, we may be able to identify new product channels and new services that address convenience as a result of going through the CLA. That's an important byproduct of the CLA. We may choose to implement a more convenient channel for our product or service as a result of this review. But it's not immediately addressable with a loyalty program.

However, suppose we believe customers see our brand and our competition at parity. Customers make the choice based on whether it's easier to turn into one parking lot or the other. If we provide a reason for customers to think twice we may get more of their business. This answer falls into the category of "addressable in a loyalty program."

The Customer

1. What do we know about sales, retention and share on a customer level?
2. Why do customers choose our brand?
3. Why do customers stay with our brand?
4. Why do customers defect from our brand?
5. Why don't customers give us all of their business?
6. What consideration process do customers go through when choosing our brand?

Many of the initial answers to these questions are similar or exactly the same across different companies and industries. I'm sure you can identify them instantly. Quality, value, price, service, selection, convenience. Ok. I've explained at least 80% of customer motivation with respect to selecting, staying, defecting and consolidating share of customer. But let's look beyond these obvious explanations. Remember that loyalty tactics are the tiebreakers that motivate customers to change behavior in small increments. We're not looking for massive shifts in behavior. Don't get me wrong, we'd love massive shifts but they're just not realistic. We must focus on small steps.

What Do We Know About Sales, Retention And Share On A Customer Level?

How much do customers buy from us in a given week, month, period, quarter, or year? Typically you have some basic segment descriptions for customers (light users, medium users, heavy users). If you're more advanced than that, great. If not, that's fine. Quite frankly, sometimes customer segmentation gets so complex it can't be used for anything anyway.

What do we know about retention rates? How long do we keep an average customer? Do we know that on a segment by segment basis? What do we know about share of customer? In other words, what percentage of a given customer's business do we get?

These are important metrics to start with. They need not be perfect answers. You may have bits and pieces from database analysis or research that you do. You may need to do a little more work to get better answers. Perhaps some additional research. But like most steps in the CLA, don't get too caught up in this one. We're not looking for absolute answers. We're looking for enough insight to allow us to formulate opinions and hypotheses.

Why Do Customers Choose Our Brand?

Think about habit. Some customers get into a habit about the way they buy goods and services. You must give them a reason to think enough about the decision to break the habit. Habit comes into play in many categories.

A brand choice is often a low involvement decision. Customers don't want to agonize over the choice. However, customers may be easily influenced if they've been given a reason to think about it. Sometimes it's a simple reason. Think about Blockbuster Rewards. It's a simple reason to pick one video rental store over another – especially when they're right across the street from one another.

Why Do Customers Stay With Our Brand?

Customers often stay with our brand because of habit. In some cases it's more difficult to defect than stay, so customers stay. Think about where your brand fits.

You may not find compelling reasons other than quality, value, price, service, selection and convenience. It's often brand failures that influence customer defection. Sometimes it's well-deployed loyalty tactics that give your brand a second chance to survive a brand failure. Customers might give you a second chance. Remember that loyal customers are more likely to complain than quietly defect.

You may have some unique heritage, tradition or legacy in your category. You might have one thing that you do that your competition doesn't. Features you identify that help influence customer defection may factor into a loyalty program. For instance, Advance Auto Parts is an automotive parts retailer in the United States. Advance Auto Parts provides a service that some of their competitors don't. They install new car batteries free. Battery installation is a dirty and potentially dangerous job. Their sales associates can do the job quickly and safely. This feature isn't expensive for Advance Auto Parts, but it's an extra benefit that gets customers more connected with sales associates. This connection is one of the reasons customers stay with the Advance Auto Parts brand.

Why Do Customers Defect From Our Brand?

Very often it's brand failures. If we're able to develop a connection with our customers, we will get some second chances to correct brand failures.

Another reason customers defect is because it's easy. If there's no reason to think much about your brand, it's easy to walk out the door or cancel service and never come back. Sometimes a loyalty program is the hook that makes customers think twice about defection.

Why Don't Customers Give Us All Of Their Business?

Convenience often comes into play here. Customers who give you some but not all of their business often represent your biggest opportunities for growth. I get a little tired of hearing about how much more expensive it is to acquire a new customer than it is to retain an existing one. Not because I don't believe it or it's not important, but because it's an isolated thought. In the grand scheme of things, companies must grow. You can't retain your way into growth, just like you can't save your way into profitability. Companies always need to acquire new customers, develop existing ones, and keep the best (those that can't possibly spend any more with your brand).

Existing customers represent an opportunity because they clearly have a relationship with your brand. It's just not as big as it could be. They buy in your category. They don't have a fundamental problem with your product or service. They're giving you some of their business. They just need a reason to give you more.

Barnes & Noble launched their Readers' Advantage program to get a greater share of their customers' business. For avid book buyers who spend a lot in the category there is no reason for them to consolidate with one brand. They need a tiebreaker that makes them do it. For example, by joining Readers' Advantage customers obtain a reason. A reason to steer clear of a Borders store in favor of the Barnes & Noble store that's down the street.

What Consideration Process Do Customers Go Through When Choosing Our Brand?

After going through the five questions that preceded this one you're likely to get a lot of redundant information. But I keep this question in the CLA process because it may occasionally shake loose something that wasn't thought of before. For instance Wendy's (a major player in the quick service restaurant business) is open until 1:00 AM in some markets while their competitors are not. It's a unique segment of their customer base that takes advantage of the late night service. There may be some ideas generated about value-added benefits tied to late night service that help strengthen the relationship between Wendy's and its

customers. Think about it. Free chili with any
order of at least $3.00 for members of Wendy's
Rewards (a fictitious program). Who can match it?

The Competition

Here we examine our competition. We review advantages
and disadvantages and we analyze what our competitors
are doing to build loyalty.

1. Who are our principal competitors?
2. What loyalty tactics does each competitor apply?
3. What are our advantages versus each competitor?
4. What are our disadvantages versus each competitor?

Who Are Our Principal Competitors?

List all the potential choices that a customer has.
Consider each alternative to your product or service.
Sometimes the choices are obvious. For instance, in
the wireless telecommunications business the
choices are limited in each market. Customers may
have a handful to choose from. However, if you're
a book retailer, the competition comes in many
forms. Supermarkets sell books. Discount retailers
sell books. Drug stores sell books. Consumers can
buy books at the mall or they can go to stand-alone
bookstores. They can also buy on-line.

What Loyalty Tactics Does Each Competitor Apply?

During your first review of this question you'll identify all the obvious things. Traditional loyalty programs that some of your competitors operate. Once you've done that, look a little bit more carefully. Loyalty tactics come in a variety of shapes and sizes.

For instance, most banks have a loyalty tactic in place that you might not think of. Internet banking. Once you've set up all your payees, your recurring payments and the various other options, you're not inclined to switch banks and go through all that work again. It's a built in loyalty tactic. You might not think about it as a loyalty tactic, but it's another hook that keeps customers with a brand.

What Are Our Advantages Versus Each Competitor?

Be honest. No company is perfect. But you may have advantages that can be leveraged in some way as loyalty tactics. I used the Advance Auto Parts example earlier. They have an advantage over some of their competitors.

What Are Our Disadvantages Versus Each Competitor?

Now put yourself into the shoes of your competition. What they have as advantages are your disadvantages.

The Communication

In this section of the CLA we're trying to get a handle on all the different ways we talk to customers. How do we speak? How do we listen? We're also looking for inconsistencies that should be corrected. Since we're planning a new marketing effort to cultivate customer loyalty it's the perfect time to ensure all our other efforts are as consistent as possible. We're also looking for inefficiencies. There's waste in every company. Including yours. Let's clean things up while we're working on programs to build customer relationships.

1. What communication tactics currently exist to facilitate customer interaction?
2. Which communication tactics are redundant?
3. Which communication tactics are inconsistent?
4. Which communication tactics are inefficient?

What Communication Tactics Currently Exist To Facilitate Customer Interaction?

This is no small task. It's helpful to make lists of the various tactics and gather samples at the same time. Once you have the various elements listed, categorized and organized, arrange them on a wall in a room that you can use on an ongoing basis as

you go through the CLA process. This room
becomes your CLA war room. When you set foot
in this room you submerge yourself in the CLA and
your brand. You now know how the customer
feels.

Look at the following categories:

- Advertising. All media. Broadcast, print, outdoor, and
  online. List the typical media selections you make for
  each.
- Product packaging.
- Brochures and other collateral. List the various ways
  pieces are typically used.
- Your website. Get a site map and, at a minimum, the
  top page of each section of your site.
- Signage, promotional banners. This depends on the
  company. Retailers often deploy in-store signs and
  banners. Consumer packaged goods companies often
  deploy special displays with signs in retail locations.
  Sprint has signs in RadioShack stores and other
  retailers. This category doesn't apply to every
  company, but I include it just to make sure we don't
  miss something.
- Direct mail. Include the typical list selection (if it's list
  driven) or database selection criteria (if it's from your
  own database). Also, include details on the results
  various campaigns have produced. Not every company
  has good documentation on results. Ideally you get to
  the point of calculating return on investment (ROI).
  But, that's an ideal world. Include whatever you have,
  no matter how subjective it may be.
- Call center contacts. List the types of calls you get
  (inbound) and the types of calls you make (outbound).

Include typical scripts and statistics on the number of each type of call you make or receive in a week, month, quarter or year.

- White mail. Identify the types of white mail do you receive from customers and how you respond.
- E-mail. Inbound and outbound. List the kind of e-mails you receive from customers and the typical responses you generate. List the kind of e-mail campaigns you initiate. Include the typical list selection (if it's list driven) or database selection criteria (if it's from your own database of e-mail addresses).

Which Communication Tactics Are Redundant?

One of the byproducts of the CLA is the identification of redundant tactics. Since we're going through our customer touch points it makes sense to look carefully for redundancy. Also, the CLA makes us look carefully at the messages we're conveying to our customers. Cultivating loyalty and building customer relationships requires smart marketing. If we do things that appear redundant, customers feel we don't have our act together and they're less likely to demonstrate loyalty to our brand.

Which Communication Tactics Are Inconsistent?

We're eliminating redundancy so let's look for inconsistency as well. Once you have all your communication components organized in the CLA war room, it's the perfect opportunity to see how consistently your message comes across through the eyes of the customer. If we're inconsistent it confuses the customer about what we really stand for as a brand.

Which Communication Tactics Are Inefficient?

Every company has waste. If you're objective about the CLA process, you'll see some tactics in the CLA war room that can be improved or eliminated.

The Operation

In this section we review our sales channels, service and support functions and potential benefits.

1.   How do we sell to customers?
2.   How do we provide service to customers and handle exceptions?
3.   What hidden benefits do we offer to customers?

How Do We Sell to Customers?

List the various channels through which customers buy our product or service. Identify the approximate percentages of sales that each channel represents of the total.

How Do We Provide Service to Customers and Handle Exceptions?

Identify the ways in which customers get help and support for the goods and services that they buy from our company. If there are multiple channels for help and support, list the approximate percentages (in terms of number of contacts) that each channel makes up of the total.

What Hidden Benefits Do We Offer to Customers?

This can be a gold mine. There are often things you do for customers that you take for granted.

I once worked with a retailer of gourmet confections. They had a policy of giving free samples (a single piece of chocolate) to customers. They never thought about it much. It was a part of their policy and their training, but they never really promoted it as a customer benefit.

RadioShack has The Repair Shop at RadioShack. Until recently it was invisible in the store. But it's a great service. You can get a wide variety of electronic devices repaired, regardless of whether or not you bought them at RadioShack.

Both of these are examples of hidden benefits. Sometimes these hidden benefits (or upgraded versions of hidden benefits) can become value-added features of a loyalty program.

The Technology

Here we review customer information. We're trying to understand how much customer information we have and where it resides. We also review how customers might be linked with purchase transactions.

1.   Do we link customers with transactions?
2.   What level of transaction information do we retain?
3.   How many different customer data sources exist within our company?

Do We Link Customers With Transactions?

A fairly basic question, but one that must be answered. With some companies this is a natural part of business. Especially with companies that bill their customers (as opposed to settling payment in other ways). Telephone companies bill customers so they already have customers linked with transaction details. Credit card companies also bill customers so they have transactions linked with customers. Retailers don't always have customers linked with transactions. If the retailer has a private label credit program in place, they'll have transactions linked with customers at least within the segment of their own credit card holders. They may also have customers linked with transactions from their on-line business, because of the need to deliver goods sold. You get the picture. Now how does it work in your business?

It's not a deal-breaker if you don't currently link customers with transactions. It will, however, probably be necessary to do so in the future so you can understand individual customer value and effectively deliver communication and benefits to customers.

If you don't link customers and transactions now, it's not all that difficult to do so. Okay. If there's a technology person reading this, he or she may be saying, "Is this guy crazy? Does he know what it takes to update all of our hardware and software?"

Yes. I do. The biggest obstacles have nothing to do with the actual work required. They have to do with making the commitment and getting the organization behind it.

What Level of Transaction Information Do We Retain?

Once we figure out the customer/transaction linkage thing, it's time to figure out what level of data we keep or might keep.

For instance, some organizations may just have a single figure that represents how much business a customer did with the company in any given day, week, month, period, quarter or year. Other companies may have each individual transaction, the product purchased, the date, the time, the location and more. And most companies are somewhere in between.

It's best to have the ability to retain as much detail as possible. It doesn't mean that you will retain the detail. It just means that you can. To make sense of customer data it must be summarized in relevant ways. If you start with details you can always summarize. However if you start with summary data you can't always get back to the detail if it's not summarized the way you need it.

How Many Different Customer Data Sources Exist Within Our Company?

Do you have five, six, seven or more different places in which customer data resides? It's not uncommon. This is an important stage of the CLA. We need to understand the location and content of existing data. But we don't want people in the organization to start developing specifications for bringing it all together before we know what we're trying to do.

The effort to integrate disparate sources of data is usually one of the most over-planned, over-engineered and under-delivered technology initiatives in the universe. And two out of three times it fails.

When you get into the integration process it's most important to take manageable steps. Figure out what information and functionality the organization needs and deliver that. Too often companies get carried away and start defining everything they would like to have. The planning process becomes more complicated than planning for a trip to the moon. And it never gets off the ground.

When You've Answered The Questions

There are two reasons to go through the CLA. First, it forces you to gather important information. Second, it forces you to go through a process that will give you great insight and wisdom about your organization, your customers and your potential options. As you go through it, some options and ideas will materialize. Jot them down as you review a variety of different loyalty options in the chapters to come.

Involving Customers in the Process

An optional but insightful step. Getting customers to be your collaborative partners in identifying your loyalty options.

These ideas involve creative methods of qualitative research (focus groups). They provide insight directly from customers who may help trigger some breakthrough ideas.

The Customer Brand Collage

This can be insightful in its ability to help you understand how customers see you today and how they would like to see you tomorrow.

Get groups of customers in a room (no more than five customers per group, no fewer than three). Have them create a collage of your brand now and your brand the way they would like it to be. Give them posterboard, a variety of magazines and catalogs. Not just things that relate to your business, but a wide variety of publications and catalogs. Give them other materials such as glue, tape, glitter, pipe cleaners and anything else you might think of for an art project.

Give the customers this simple direction: Using the materials you have, create a collage on one board that represents the way you see us today. Create a collage on a second board that represents the way you would like to see us. That's it. Give them an hour or an hour and a half to work on it. Then ask them to provide a brief explanation of their work to one person (you don't want to force customers to give a major presentation to you and your entire marketing staff). Videotape the explanation if possible.

Have customers develop loyalty programs concepts

This is a more direct tactic. Keep in mind that when you start talking about loyalty ideas with customers, they will often tell you to "just lower your prices." The first thing to do is get beyond that. If the price topic comes up, just tell customers to assume that sweeping price reductions are not viable.

Have groups of three to five customers create concepts for a customer loyalty program. Have each group create just one. Have them list the features of the program. Have each group explain the concept to one person and videotape it if possible.

Create a customer advisory board

This is more of an ongoing way to get customer guidance and insight. Create a board of customer advisors. This may be a large group that never actually meets together, but meets separately in smaller groups. For instance you might have a few dozen members in each of your key markets. You have a meeting every month or so (in one of your markets) with a group of local advisors. You have a discussion with your advisors about your business and their thoughts and ideas. Once you have a loyalty program in place, this advisory group can be a customer steering committee that helps you keep the program vibrant and relevant. Be sure to have a way of disseminating information regularly to this group (newsletters, bulletins, e-mails, a special website).

The CLA is an insightful process. It provides tremendous information that will be essential as you consider options for implementing loyalty tactics.

Chapter Six

Loyalty Marketing
In Practice

There are many ways to achieve customer loyalty. As we look at options I'm going to refer to "forks in the road." A fork in the road is a decision we must make. It's a choice about the best path. It's an informed decision based on your assessment of readiness (the extent to which your house is in order) and the results of your CLA.

Defined Programs versus Contact Strategies

The first fork in the road.

A defined program has structure. Take a look back at MCI's program called Free Flix. It has structure. Spend $25 and get a free video rental. Spend $50 and get two video rentals. And so on.

Many of the programs I've described earlier in this book are defined programs. Typically, defined programs are the easiest for marketers and consumers to identify. The alternative – a contact strategy – is not quite as easy to identify. Not because it's difficult to see, but because we just don't think about it as an approach to developing customer loyalty.

A contact strategy consists of a planned series of customer communication programs that often vary by customer segment. On the receiving end, customers react to each communication component as an isolated marketing communication tactic. They might think, "Oh, yeah, I get things in the mail or e-mail from them." They don't think about it as a program.

Behind the scenes, through the eyes of the marketer, it is a program. It's a carefully considered, methodically planned program. It may be as successful or more successful than a defined program. I'm not saying that one is better than the other. You should consider both as you navigate this fork in the road toward evaluating your loyalty options.

Announced versus Clandestine Programs

The next fork in the road. This consideration – announced or clandestine – applies only to defined programs, not contact strategies.

An announced program is just that - announced. A customer can find out about it fairly easily. It's promoted and explained at your website. It's integrated in your advertising. It's in everything you do. You can't miss it.

An announced program is difficult to measure in a traditional direct marketing sense. Pure measurement involves holding out a random control group that is consistent in composition to your test group. It's not possible to hold out a control group when the program is available for customers to enroll at will.

A clandestine program is privately communicated to a group of customers, usually through the mail or e-mail. You select the customers and you also establish the control group. Clandestine programs can be measured more effectively because you are able to hold out a control group. However, with a clandestine program you cannot evaluate the overall potential of your program. For instance, if Blockbuster tested its Rewards program clandestinely, they would not have been able to evaluate the impact of having the program integrated with advertising and point of sale posters. They also would not have been able to evaluate the impact of having a sales associate say, "Are you familiar with Blockbuster Rewards?"

Hard Benefits

A hard benefit is one that is typically a percentage of a customer's spending. The more you spend, the more you get. Hard benefits come in two flavors: promotional currency and discounts.

A promotional currency is a system of value earned and redeemed in a loyalty program. It goes by many different names (points and miles are fairly common names). It's typically a percentage of a customer's spending.

Promotional currency is not the only way to structure a loyalty program. Unfortunately, whenever the term "loyalty program" is used, it causes marketing people to instantly think of points for free stuff.

The promotional currency model has its share of complexities and idiosyncrasies. I'll spend the entire next chapter going into more detail about the important planning considerations that revolve around it.

Some hard benefits programs use discounts instead of promotional currency. For instance, the Barnes & Noble Readers' Advantage program gives members a 10% discount. The Waldenbooks Preferred Reader program has both forms of hard benefits. Members get 10% off on their spending and they also earn one point for every dollar spent. Once a member accumulates 100 points, it converts to a five dollar reward certificate.

Soft Benefits

Soft benefits are extra benefits, available to customers, that are not a percentage of spending. It doesn't mean they're free. It just means they're not a direct function of spending.

However, certain soft benefits may be made available to customers once they have spent a certain amount. The most common soft benefits to talk about are some of those in the airline industry. Upgrades, shorter lines.

Barnes & Noble offers soft benefits to its Readers' Advantage members. They hold special literary events only for members. Blockbuster offers several soft benefits in its Rewards program. Members get a free favorite rental each month and a free favorite on certain days of the week with a paid rental.

Soft benefits can also be unexpected benefits. Unanticipated things you do for a customer based on what you know about the customer's relationship with you.

Here's a nice example of an unexpected soft benefit. It's not in conjunction with a defined or announced program. In fact it's probably part of a clandestine contact strategy that also includes unexpected soft benefits.

Here's the story. It's about the Adolphus Hotel in Dallas, Texas. I checked in a few months ago. Before this, I had probably stayed at the Adolphus six or eight times in the previous three years. They did not have a loyalty program that I participated in.

It was late. I pulled up, valet-parked my rental car, and checked in. Nothing special.

I carried my own bag to the elevator and proceeded to the fifth floor. I got off the elevator and headed for my room. When I arrived at my room, a room service staff member greeted me at the door and said "Mr. Duffy, I have something for you."

He followed me in my room and presented me with a tray. The tray had a bottle of sparkling water, a slice of pound cake with flavored butter and a strawberry.

Along with the tray was a card. The server introduced it as
a message for me. It was a small, handwritten envelope,
with my name on it. The pre-printed part of the card said:

> "Welcome back to the Adolphus! We take great
> pride in your loyalty and look forward to being your
> host on this occasion.
>
> Your comments and suggestions would be most
> appreciated.
>
> With kindest regards,"
>
> Greg Champion
> Managing Director

The note was hand signed by Greg Champion.

It was a nice touch. It impressed me. They never promised
me a benefit like this so it caught me off guard. It made a
lasting impression.

Developing Soft Benefits

If you're going to have announced soft benefits in a
program, it's best not to have too many. A couple of soft
benefits is fine. Five to seven is probably the maximum.
After seven it begins to look like you're trying too hard.
People begin to think you weren't impressed with the
quality of your benefits so you focused on quantity.

Here's how to develop your own list of potential soft
benefits. First, look at customer suggestions and

complaints. They're often a good source of ideas. Second, look at the hidden benefits that you identified during the CLA. Finally, get a group of people together and brainstorm ideas. Use the customer suggestions and complaints as well as the hidden benefits to stimulate the discussion. Get as many ideas as possible. Don't shoot any down. That comes later.

Regroup at least one day after you've brainstormed the initial ideas. Review the ideas and filter out those that seem financially or operationally impossible. Take the remaining ideas and do some basic research. Get customers to rank order the potential benefits. Once that's complete, do a thorough operational and financial review to ascertain the complexity and cost of each one. At this point you'll have a fairly good handle on the winners and losers. You'll be able to make your choices and move on.

Communication

Communication is an essential component of a loyalty program. In fact, depending upon what you choose to do, communication might be the loyalty program.

Before exploring communication tactics, let's touch on strategy for a minute. Your loyalty program is a brand under the umbrella of your master brand. It must support and enhance your master brand. It should never conflict with your master brand. It should express something special. Consider how you want your customers to feel after they receive and experience your communication. Develop a brand strategy and a communication strategy for your program before jumping into tactics.

Getting the Word Out and Enrolling Customers

This section applies only to defined programs. Your approach will vary based on whether it's announced or clandestine. Once you've got your program defined, how will you tell customers? And whom will you tell?

While some programs solicit membership via a direct mail or e-mail invitation, other programs simply assume customers in and welcome them. Some announced programs are featured in advertising campaigns for the master brand. The program becomes another reason to visit the master brand. This is becoming increasingly common with grocery store chains.

Some programs are completely voluntary – advertising, collateral and web-site tell the story about the program, and customers must volunteer or self-select to become members.

If you're inviting customers to become members, consider multiple campaigns. Test e-mail versus traditional direct mail. Some customers just won't understand what you're trying to tell them the first time around, or they won't pay attention. Follow-up communication efforts are almost always worth the effort and expense.

If you automatically enroll customers and welcome them through the mail or e-mail, many of them (typically about two-thirds) will ignore your welcome and will have no idea that they're even members. If you conduct research to understand program awareness or recall after a single announcement, you might be disappointed. With ongoing communication, the awareness and recall will consistently rise. Be realistic and remember that your program is a new brand. It takes time and frequent impressions to build a memorable brand.

If your front-line employees have interaction with customers and will play a role in communicating your program, don't short-cut training and employee communication. Your customers are sure to become skeptical quickly if they find that your employees are untrained, confused, or apathetic about your loyalty program.

Enrollment Fees

Some programs charge membership fees. If you're considering doing so, think long and hard about it.

Your program must have value that is instantly apparent. Your brand must be a high utility brand – one that customers use often. Look at the companies that get fees for their programs. Blockbuster, Barnes & Noble, Musicland, Waldenbooks and MCI (Frequent Flyer Rewards). Each program has high utility and delivers a value proposition that makes it realistic to assume customers will pay. Make sure you're in the same situation before deciding to attach a fee to membership.

Welcome

When you've enrolled a customer, it's important to follow up and confirm or acknowledge the enrollment. Whether it's an e-mail, a letter, a welcome card or a welcome kit, it's essential to acknowledge the new relationship.

Information Gathering

Don't get carried away trying to gather excessive information when a customer enrolls in your program. Too often companies are tempted to include a bunch of questions without even knowing what they'll do with the answers. The more difficult you make it to enroll, the lower your enrollment rates. Don't over complicate things. You can always go back later and get customers to respond to surveys and information requests. Keep the enrollment process clean.

Ongoing Communication

Once you have the word out and you're beginning to build momentum, you'll need some ongoing communication tactics to keep customers informed and engaged.

Some companies decide to use newsletters. Whether they're traditional printed newsletters or e-mail newsletters, make sure you know what you're getting into. Think ahead more than one issue. Think into next year. Many newsletter efforts die after the first issue for two reasons: 1) the company runs out of content or; 2) the company runs out of money.

Develop your communication strategy in advance. Deliver a blend of information about your brand and your program. Try to get customers to opt-in to e-mail communication. The e-mail channel allows you to communicate more frequently and cost-effectively.

Communication and Education as a Soft Benefit

There are situations in which communication can become a soft benefit. When communication provides relevant education that helps the customer, it becomes a soft benefit.

I've seen communication in the form of "how to" information used as a soft benefit in the home improvement retail category. By providing useful information to customers, home improvement retailers boost sales. They teach people to take on projects. Customers take on more complex projects than they previously thought possible. The result - they buy more tools, equipment and supplies.

I've also seen it work in the telecommunications industry. Customers (this applies to both consumers and businesses) often cancel specific telecommunications products because they feel like they're not getting enough value. This value deficiency is often linked to customers not knowing how to use a product. By providing educational communication, some telecommunications companies have reduced product defection rates. They teach customers how to use their product. Customers use the product more and feel like they're getting better value.

Now that we've reviewed loyalty marketing in practice, it's time to take a closer look at the promotional currency model. It's complex but powerful.

Chapter Seven

Promotional Currency Model Explored

Points. Miles. Whatever.

The promotional currency model of loyalty has its own unique set of considerations. Don't underestimate the complexity of this. I don't mean to scare you away. A promotional currency program can be a very effective way to keep customers. It can also become a powerful platform for launching other promotional marketing activities. But like all great things, it comes at a price. The price is measured in money, effort and commitment.

The first consideration is this. How will a member be identified?

Membership Cards And Tags

Will you issue membership cards? Key chain tags (quite popular these days)? Do you already link customers with transactions? This is an important question and along with it go the questions of logistics.

If customers are going to get a card or tag, how do they get it? Temporary cards are sometimes attached to membership applications and customers are able to enroll and participate instantly. In the temporary membership card situation, you wait until the member has had a couple of transactions, then you mail a permanent card and/or tag. In other programs, permanent identification materials are issued on the spot, also allowing customers to enroll and participate instantly.

There are cost trade-offs with the two methods I've outlined above. With temporary cards followed by permanent cards in the mail, you have the mailing cost. With permanent cards issued on the spot you ultimately waste more expensive materials.

There are certainly other ways. Just about every program should have an on-line enrollment function. You can issue a member number and even allow members to print their own temporary card (complete with bar code) instantly.

Name Your Promotional Currency

The currency might be referred to as "points" or "miles." I've seen other terms used as well. On several occasions, I've seen the term "credits." And for a golf course, I saw the term "yards." Some companies try communicating their currency in percentages of spending, hoping to avoid naming the currency -"You'll earn 1% on all purchases, but on Tuesdays you'll earn a 50% bonus or 1.5%." This can get confusing, especially when you try to introduce a bonus: "You'll earn 1% plus you'll get an extra $5.00 credit on Fridays."

For the sake of clarity it's important to name your currency.

Select an Appropriate Unit of Measure

The unit of measure should not be too large nor too small. As a rule of thumb, a promotional currency should be worth one cent on the redemption side of the equation. That's large enough so that members aren't throwing around tens- or hundreds-of-thousands of points for $25 in value. But it's also small enough that you can work out bonuses or partnership deals that don't require splitting points into fractions. Let me illustrate:

Suppose you've decided that a five percent funding rate is appropriate for your situation. You announce that members will earn one point for every dollar spent and that each point is worth five cents (for a real example of this precise funding model, see the Waldenbooks Preferred Reader program). Next you make a deal with a partner company. The partner company can't afford five percent, but they can afford two percent. It's still a good deal that adds value to your relationship with your customers. Since the partner will pay you for the currency, you make a deal. Now you'll have to tell your members they'll earn 40% of one point for every dollar spent or one point for every $2.50 spent with your partner. If the currency is worth one cent, you can tell members they'll earn five points for every dollar spent with you and two points for every dollar spent with your partner.

Require Redemption in Fixed Units

Requiring members to redeem points in denominations that you define will virtually guarantee that they will always have a balance remaining after redeeming. Therefore, they will be reluctant to defect because they will always have something to lose. Having this structure will ensure that all of your promotional currency can never be redeemed.

Here's an example. Let's use the Waldenbooks Preferred Reader program as the example. Members earn one point for every dollar spent (in addition to their ten percent instant discount). Once a member has accumulated 100 points, a five-dollar reward is issued. Let's say I had 80 points and just made a purchase for $35. Now I have 115 points. They deduct 100 points, send me a five-dollar reward, but I still have 15 points in the bank. I'm on my way to my next reward and if I don't go back to Waldenbooks and give them more business, I'm leaving value on the table. That's an economic cost of defection – making customers think twice about leaving.

Using Redemption to Drive Sales

Most promotional currency programs have several options on the redemption side. A few years back, many companies – regardless of industry – offered a catalog of merchandise and some travel-related options for redemption. These basic offerings evolved from the incentive and motivation business. Over time, most marketers (especially on the consumer side) found these redemption options too expensive to offer for their customer marketing programs. Today, most programs like this offer a redemption option for the marketer's own product (for instance, most retailers with promotional currency programs offer redemption in the form of gift certificates).

Ultimately, redemption should be used to drive incremental sales. After all, the primary objective of loyalty marketing is to improve retention and increase share of customer. These objectives are measured in terms of larger average sales per customer. Sometimes, a gift certificate may displace a paid sale because the customer would have shopped anyway. But with careful analysis regarding a customer's average time between purchases, you can set an expiration date on a redemption gift certificate to help ensure that the sales are incremental.

For instance, if your research shows that the average time between visits to the store is 60 days, set the expiration date for 30 days and automatically trigger the award. When a customer shops and clears the necessary plateau, generate the award and mail it (or e-mail it) to the customer. Since the customer just shopped, the 30-day expiration date will ensure that if the certificate is used before the expiration, the sale can be considered incremental.

Here's an example of a program that probably could have been more aggressive about their expiration dates. The McDonald's Road2Rewards program issued rewards with an expiration date about 75 days after the redemption cutoff date (because this was a short test program, all rewards appear to have had the same expiration date). Any member who earned a reward is probably coming in at least one a month. With a 75 day expiration period, the reward (if it's a reward for McDonald's food) is unlikely to generate incremental activity. It will just cannibalize an otherwise paid transaction. However, if McDonald's made the expiration period shorter – say 21 days after the estimated "in home" date – they'd have a better chance of generating incremental business.

Some say this approach is manipulative. But if you do not build mechanisms into your loyalty program to ensure that you improve your business, you'll merely reward existing business and drive up your cost structure.

The Program Accounting System

This is no small task. Don't mistake your marketing database or your data warehouse for a program accounting system. This is a different animal. There are companies who sell software packages or packaged services to support the program accounting system for loyalty programs. Some companies decide they'll do it themselves with internal development resources. Often this is a company culture consideration. I've been in companies that always decide to build something rather than buy it. Some companies are just "do it yourself" companies. So be it. If you're one of those companies, just make sure the information technology team you're working with has the right level of passion to do this.

Basic Program Accounting System Information

The major information components are members and transactions. When a customer enrolls and becomes a member, you create a member record. As a member transacts with your program, you post transactions to the member's account.

What I've described below is the information you'll need for a basic program accounting system. This is simplified to some degree and I'm sure many readers can suggest other things that are necessary for certain situations. Every company's needs vary. But what I've laid out probably addresses the information required to manage 90% of the situations you'll face.

Members

Some key elements you'll need to include in a member record:

- Member number. Some identification number you'll use to link a member's information together. If you're already tracking customer information you'll have some identification number (probably called a customer number). If you don't and all this customer data is new to you, you'll need to establish a number scheme. No big deal, but it's just something you'll need to do.
- Name, address, city, state, zip code, phone number, e-mail address. The basic mailing and communication information. If it's a business-to-business program, you'll need a company name and title for the contact person who is the member.
- Enrollment date. You'll want to keep track of when the customer became a member. This is a useful piece of information to have, especially if you want to recognize tenure within the program.

- Enrollment method. An indication of how the customer became a member. On-line enrollment. Off-line enrollment. You'll have your own definitions based on the kind of business you're in and the nature of your program.
- Preferred communication method. Does the member prefer to receive communication in the mail, via e-mail, or not at all?
- Member status. You'll probably want to define some status codes to assign to members. Some of the most basic ones are "Active" and "Inactive" to reflect how long it's been since the member has had activity. There are no universal definitions for active and inactive, but you'll probably find it useful to define something for your business even if you need to change it later on. You may also have a status for things like "Undeliverable" for those who don't have a mailable address and "No Contact" for those who don't want to receive mail or e-mail.
- Current balance. The current balance in the member's promotional currency account.

These are the fundamentals for a member record. There are other summary statistics you'll want to carry for members, but they typically exist in something that might be called a "Member Summary" record. The member record is the contact information that allows us to understand a member's basic status and contact information.

Transactions

Transactions include member purchases and redemption transactions. This is a running tally of the transactions that affect the member's promotional currency balance. Purchases add to the member's balance. Redemption transactions reduce the member's balance.

Below I've identified some key elements you'll need in transactions. This is a little more difficult than describing member information because this tends to get even more specific based on the type of business you're in. If your business has multiple line items on each transaction you may have a transaction number that ties various records together. Transactions may have a header record and accompanying detail records that collectively describe the transaction. That's a slightly more complex situation than the one I've outlined below, but once you have a sense of how this works it's not a tremendous leap to get to that level.

- Member number. This will link the transaction back to the member.
- Date/time of transaction.
- Type of transaction. This may vary based on your business. Some universal types may be "Purchase" and "Redemption." Some other types you may find necessary include "Return" (if you're in the kind of business that has returns that create customer credits) and "Adjustment" (there are always things that need to be adjusted).

- Location. Depending on your business. In retailing this might be a store number. In the hotel business it might be a hotel number. If you're in a multi-channel business (off-line, on-line, catalog) the location code might indicate the channel through which the transaction occurred.
- Amount of transaction. This is simplified. Depending upon your business, you may have sales tax, delivery charges and other amount categories that you'll carry in this record. The important thing is this: keep the amount fields at all times. There is also a "Base Currency Earned" field and I've seen people drop the original dollar amount and just carry the calculated currency. If you have to trace a transaction back to its roots to investigate potential errors it becomes very difficult if you don't have the original amount fields.
- Base currency earned. Based on the rules of your program, how much the member earned for this transaction.
- Bonus currency earned. This is populated based on any bonuses in effect at the time the transaction occurred. You may also have a bonus code that explains why the bonus occurred. For instance, if you're a restaurant chain and you're offering a 50% bonus on transactions that occur between 2:00 PM and 4:00 PM there might be a unique code to describe that. Let's say you make the same bonus 100% on Tuesdays because they're particularly slow. That might be a different code.

That is the most basic information required to track transactions.

Member Summary

A member summary record is one that holds cumulative buckets of information that allow you to have a snapshot of your relationship with each member. I will suggest some categories for the buckets, but often the same buckets occur over and over again for different time periods. For instance you might have a "Total Transactions" bucket for each of the last 12 months (or 13 periods if you're a 13 period company).

Some ideas for member summary information:

- Member number.
- Date & amount of most recent transaction. This information (and the next two suggestions) allows a quick look at recency of activity and size of recent transactions.
- Date & amount of second most recent transaction.
- Date & amount of third most recent transaction.
- Average transaction amount over the past year.
- Average days between transactions over the past year.
- Total transactions (12 buckets, current month and prior 11).
- Total spending (12 buckets, current month and the prior 11).
- Currency earned (12 buckets, current month and prior 11).
- Currency redeemed (12 buckets, current month and prior 11).

The member summary is a handy snapshot of
member behavior. It's used as a decision support
tool and a selection tool for targeted marketing
activities. Even if you find you need new summary
statistics over time, no problem. Change the way
you summarize and redefine the variables. This is
created from member transactions, so you can
summarize it any way you like.

There are other potential summaries you may find
useful. I've seen member/location summaries in the
retail and hotel business, providing a snapshot of
the relationship between a member and a location.
If it's in the transaction records, you can use it to
create useful summaries. These summaries help
facilitate your understanding of customer dynamics
and your execution of targeted and measurable
marketing activities.

Basic Program Accounting System Functionality

We've reviewed basic information requirements, now let's
take a look at basic functional requirements.

Enrollment

You'll need to have the functionality to set up a new
member. This may happen several ways. You
might have enrollment forms that are filled out by
customers and shipped off someplace for data entry.
The enrollment process might be integrated at point
of sale – customers join, the name and address entry
happens right then. You may also have on-line
enrollment. Customers go to your website, input

their information and become members. You might have an opt-in process. You mail an invitation to customers and they phone your call center or visit your website to tell you "Yes." In this case, you already have an electronic record with their contact information and you're probably just going to ask them for a member number to activate their account (and perhaps ask them for an e-mail address).

Inquiry

You'll need functionality to look up a member's account, check transaction activity and the current balance. Depending on your program, you may have a call center (or a special group within an existing call center) to handle program related customer inquiries. Those agents may use this functionality to answer questions and solve problems.

The majority of inquiries revolve around, "What's my balance?" Build into the system a web-deployed look up function so customers can register and check their balance online. Consider an interactive voice response feature to allow members to check their balance over the phone (but without a live agent).

Redemption

There are two forms of redemption: automatic and voluntary. With automatic redemption, a reward of some type (a certificate – paper or electronic) is generated and delivered to the member when their balance hits a certain level. With voluntary redemption, a member's balance continues to grow until the member contacts the program to redeem.

With automatic redemption, the process is fairly straightforward. You run a process every day, week or whatever. The process picks members who are above the redemption threshold, creates a reward for them, and creates a redemption transaction, thus reducing the member's balance.

With voluntary redemption, it may be a process that the member initiates over the web, in person, over the phone, via fax or through the mail. The transaction process is much like I've described for automatic redemption.

Adjustments

Remember when I described an "Adjustment" transaction type? Well this is where it's used. Agents need to fix things and that's how they do it.

When a member calls up and says they're missing a transaction or they didn't get the right amount of currency, no problem. Fix it. Don't haggle or go into excessive probing. Believe them and fix it. You'll occasionally find people who are cheating the system. Build in controls so you can identify any member who calls more than two or three times with the same story. Spend your time looking into the exceptions, not the norms.

Combining Accounts

When you define your program, develop a policy to address this. Most programs at some point need the functionality to take all of the transactions from two different accounts and make them one.

That's a look at the basic functionality you'll need. Start with this framework and customize it to suit your company's needs. Or look at some of the standardized solutions available in the marketplace. Whatever you do, don't underestimate the task.

Accounting

A few final considerations. There are accounting implications when you're looking at a promotional currency program. I'm going to walk you through the basic accounting transactions that are used to keep the books.

When members transact with your program, you set aside (or reserve) part of the revenue to account for future redemption. If you have a five percent funded program, you theoretically set aside five percent. I say theoretically because that's the worst-case scenario. When we get into the measurement chapter we'll have some fun with math and explore the conversion of a gross funding rate into a net funding rate.

Here's a look at the basic debit and credit entries. These entries occur in addition to the accounting transactions that you currently record to recognize revenue.

There are two new general ledger accounts I'll describe.
One is "Program Funding Expense." It represents the
amount you're setting aside on each transaction to pay for
future redemption. This is either an expense account or a
contra-revenue account. It either increases expenses or
reduces revenues. The bottom line impact is the same, but
depending on how your CFO and/or auditors choose to
record it, it may have different affects on ratios.

The second new account is "Reserve for Program
Redemption." This is the liability you've probably heard
about. It appears on your balance sheet and it represents
the total amount you owe customers. It's a close cousin to
the "Accounts Payable" line on your balance sheet.
Accounts Payable represents the amount you owe suppliers.
Reserve for Program Redemption represents the amount
you owe customers.

When a customer buys something:

Debit   Program Funding Expense

      Credit   Reserve for Program Redemption

When a customer redeems something:

Debit   Reserve for Program Redemption

      Credit   Cash (or some other account)

This second one is somewhat simplistic but it gets at the
essence. Some of it is a function of how you currently
account for sales. I've laid out this basic accounting
information so you can facilitate a discussion with your

accounting and finance leaders to see how you'll handle this component of a loyalty program.

Now that we've taken a thorough look at the promotional currency model, let's review segmentation and contact strategy.

Chapter Eight

Segmentation And Contact Strategy

There's more than one way to achieve loyalty. I took you through the nuts and bolts of the promotional currency model in the previous chapter. Segmentation and contact strategy is another option.

The segmentation and contact strategy approach doesn't typically require the same commitment as a promotional currency program. You're not making a promise to customers. You might be making a promise to yourself and to your company.

This approach assumes you have customers linked with transactions. Companies that do not have the customer/transaction linkage might launch promotional currency programs to create the linkage. If not a promotional currency program, they'll create a discount program that requires customers to carry and use an identification mechanism. The Readers' Advantage program at Barnes & Noble falls into this category. Many grocery store chain programs also fall into this category.

Segmentation

This is not a book about segmentation. That's a good thing. An entire book on segmentation might be just a little boring.

I'm going to focus on some basic segmentation approaches. If you're not using segmentation to drive a contact strategy, chances are you should start fairly simply anyway. Don't underestimate simplicity and common sense.

Segmentation is a way to group customers. I'm focusing on ways to group customers based on their past behavior, not on demographics or anything else. If you haven't done much of this in your company the best place to start is always with past transaction data.

Segmentation Dimensions

Segmentation dimensions are the elements you use to discriminate different groups of customers. One of the most common sets of segmentation definitions is RFM. RFM stands for Recency, Frequency and Monetary Value. Here's what they mean:

> **Recency**. How recent a customer's last transaction was. You might calculate this in absolute days and assign a score to each customer to indicate if they're in the top third, middle third, or bottom third of the entire customer base. I used thirds just as an

example. You can also do it in tenths (deciles) or quarters (quartiles). You can do it any way you want. It's your data. But this is my book, so I did it in thirds. It's a simple place to start.

Frequency. How often a customer has a transaction. There are at least two ways to look at this. One is to calculate average number of transactions in a period of time (quarter, year). The other is to calculate a mean time between transactions (MTBT). Both approaches get at the same thing. Typically you assign a score to this just like you did with recency.

Monetary value. How much a customer spends in a period of time (quarter, year). Calculate a score.

If you've done each dimension in thirds, you'll have a three by three by three cube. You'll have 27 different segments. Take each segment and calculate some basic metrics such as:

- Average number of transactions (in a given period) or MTBT
- Average spending (in a period)
- Average transaction size

This allows you to logically group customers and understand their relative value. I've used some very simple metrics. Ultimately it's good to get into contribution margin, or gross profit metrics. If you overlay demographic characteristics on customer records it allows you to get a better sense of who the customers are. I find demographics are better for adding texture to your segments. Actual transaction data is better for defining the segments.

RFM is a very common approach. Let's look at some variations. These are all cousins of RFM, but they might yield better insight depending upon your business. Here are some dimensions you might want to look at.

Tenure. How long has a customer been with your brand? We all hear about how 80% of our business comes from 20% of our customers (although it's rarely really 80/20). But are they really the same 20%? Not in all businesses. Do you know the extent to which it's true in yours? Long tenure says something about a customer. You have a durable relationship with a customer who has been with you for a long period of time.

Breadth of transactions. This depends on your business. If you sell many lines of products or services, it indicates the extent to which a given customer uses many or few of your products. Breadth says something about a customer. It says the customer understands what you're about as a brand.

Channel use. This depends on whether or not you have multiple channels through which customers may buy. The most common pair of channels is off-line and on-line. Customers who only buy off-line are likely to be quite different from those who only buy on-line. You probably have more single transaction customers in the on-line only channel. There is typically more trial in on-line businesses.

Customers who fall into the category of both, are probably more engaged with your brand.

There may be other dimensions unique to your business. But this provides a place to start. I've suggested six different dimensions, with some inter-relationships between them. I would not suggest using them all together when you start. Focus on a few that seem to make sense for your business and add complexity as you go.

Developing a Contact Strategy

Go back to everything you discovered in the CLA. Especially insights about why customers select and reject your brand. Why they stay and why they defect. This will help you develop ideas for your contact strategy.

For example, suppose you're a gourmet food retailer and you discover during the CLA that your customers think about your brand principally for themselves. They buy your products for self-consumption. You identify an opportunity to position your brand as a source for gifts. This repositioning may be an overall theme for your contact strategy.

Developing Objectives

We want to develop objectives for each segment. If you have 27 segments (as our first example did) you might think about collapsing some of them together for the sake of establishing objectives. You can look at all 27 segments when you're doing the analysis, but you don't necessarily need to define objectives for each one (because it's likely that many objectives will look similar). If you're starting with the RFM segmentation, just look at the F and the M (frequency and monetary value). That makes it a three by three matrix (nine segments) for the sake of defining objectives.

Now let's set some objectives. We're going to set objectives for a year, and measure our results, by segment, over the course of the year. We'll review some of the measurement approaches in a later chapter. There are several categories of objectives:

> **Revenue growth**. By getting customers to consolidate more of their business with you (share of customer growth), you'll see increased revenue. You'll be able to determine whether that growth is from increased frequency or increased transaction size. Set objectives as a percentage. For instance, a revenue growth objective might be to increase revenue by 15% in all segments.

> **Improved retention**. By communicating with customers in a methodical, meaningful and relevant way, you should see an improvement in retention. Set objectives as an improvement in the retention rate in each segment. For instance, a retention objective might be to improve retention rate in segment one by five percentage points.

> **Changes in perceptions about the brand**. These are objectives that will be measured with research, not with customer transaction data. Things such as increases in unaided awareness. Likelihood to choose your brand first in the category. Likelihood to complain rather than quietly defect. These are important objectives that point to the future. They

help indicate changes in the long-term impression the customer has about the brand. These impressions may lead to long-term loyalty.

Developing Budgets

The budgets you develop for a contact strategy can be linked directly with the business improvements you'll create. However, the business improvements may not completely materialize in the short run (the first year) because you'll need to do some testing. When you're testing, you often have fixed costs that are spread across relatively small groups of customers. The cost per customer is high and the resultant return on investment (ROI) doesn't look good. However, things improve when you spread the costs over the larger quantities of customers when you roll out your efforts.

Good contact strategies can yield a 10% to 25% lift in sales. You must spend money to get that lift. I've seen effective contact strategies that generate 25% to 100% ROI. Using this information, you can develop a proposed budget.

Let's assume the following for the sake of this example:

- The customers you're going to include in your contact strategy represent $25 million in annual sales.
- Your gross profit is 40%.
- You can consistently generate a 50% ROI on your contact strategy spending.
- You can generate a 15% lift with your contact strategy.

The results are on the following page.

Base Sales	$ 25,000,000
Lift @ 15%	$ 28,750,000
Incremental Gross Profit @ 40%	$ 1,500,000
Spending required at 50% ROI	$ 1,000,000

You spend one million dollars. You generate $1.5 million in incremental gross profit. That's based on a number of assumptions. This is an approach for developing a starting point. You'll need to factor in your own assumptions and other unique circumstances about your business.

If one million dollars is your rollout budget, you'll probably need 25% to 50% of that during the testing phase. You won't be achieving the 50% ROI or the 15% lift across the board. You'll probably need to go through six months to a year of testing to get to optimal levels. Then you'll need to do periodic re-testing to ensure that you're always improving your contact strategy efforts. It's a journey, not a destination.

Developing Programs

You have segments, objectives and budgets. Now we need to do some marketing. Remember that we're not talking about defined or announced programs. We're not talking about hard benefit programs. We're talking about communication and, potentially, unexpected benefits. The media may be traditional direct mail and e-mail. E-mail is obviously much less expensive, but it's not necessarily more effective. You'll need to test with your customers in your situation.

Your ideas will be stimulated by your segment dimensions, your discoveries from the CLA, and your experience and intuition. Let me suggest some ideas.

- Recognition for highest spending customers. A thank you message. An exclusive offer. I worked with a retailer that offered a "no strings attached" free gift. Customers picked up the free gift at point of sale and almost half of them made a purchase along with it.
- Stimulation programs for customers who have high average transactions. These are very often your most profitable customers. Even small incremental response rates generate large ROI.
- Education programs for customers who only buy from one of your lines of business. Teach customers about all you offer. Leverage the passion they have for your brand into other areas of your business.
- Referral programs. Ask your good customers to introduce their friends and relatives to your brand.
- Reactivate dormant customers. Test algorithms for defining dormancy. Test offers for reactivating.
- New customer development programs. If you can engage with a customer early in the process, you may improve the size and duration of the relationship.

Those are some jump-start ideas. Combine those with your thoughts and you'll be on your way to defining the first version of your contact strategy. Start by allocating your budgets evenly across your segments. I used three by three segmentation examples because it's easy to grasp and manage. Start by allocating one third of your budget to the lowest monetary band, one third to the middle and one third to the top. After some testing you'll begin to get a sense of where your biggest opportunities for ROI are.

Chapter Nine

The Right Choice
For Your Business

We've been through plenty of examples, methodologies and approaches. Let's take a look at how to make a decision for your business.

I'll share some tools that you can use to make choices. Each tool provides a way of looking at your business and where it fits. Once you see where your business fits, you'll see some suggestions about the approaches that might work for you. The ultimate choice is yours. There won't be black and white recommendations, just shades of gray.

Nature of Goods and Services

First, let's think about how much our customers really like
our product. Do they buy our product because they like it?
Do they buy our product because it's something they need
for every day life? Do they buy our product only because
they absolutely must?

Take a look at some basic categories of goods and services
and where they fit in the Attitude/Behavior Model:

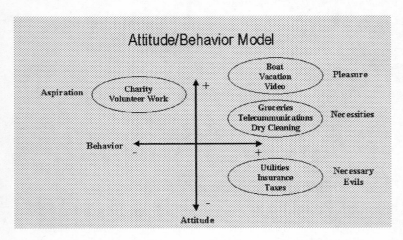

The Attitude/Behavior Model helps you understand how
customers see and use your product. The vertical axis is
customer attitude: how they feel about your product. The
horizontal axis is behavior: how customers behave with
your product. Understanding this will help you think about
the extent to which your solution is fun and exciting, or
serious and businesslike. It will also help you keep things
in perspective.

Transaction Velocity and Size

Let's look at the average price of the product or service you sell and the velocity at which customers buy. I have organized things into four quadrants, based on two dimensions. Purchase velocity is frequent and infrequent. Frequent velocity means the mean time between transaction (MTBT from the previous chapter) is less than one year. Infrequent means the MTBT is one year or greater. Purchase amount is divided into high and low. In U.S. Dollars, high is $100 or more. Low is less than $100.

Let's illustrate this by taking a look at some typical products and where they fit in the velocity and size model:

Transaction Velocity and Size

	Infrequent	Frequent
High $	Boat Vehicle Vacation Appliance	Airline Tickets Credit Card Transactions Apparel White Tablecloth Dining Groceries Phone Service
Low $	Baking Soda Toothpicks Ketchup	Apparel Casual Dining Oil Change Gasoline Music Purchase Video Rental

Put your product or service into this model and determine
where it fits. Once you've done that, take a look at the
following graphic that illustrates some of the potential
approaches.

Transaction Velocity and Size

	Infrequent	Frequent
High $	- Gauge customer satisfaction - Ensure brand presence - Reinforce brand characteristics - Anticipate readiness to buy	- Recognize/reward status - Develop/deliver soft benefits - Communicate special values - Maximize share of customer
Low $	- Co-op programs - Brand building - Distribution - Promotion - Communicate new uses	- Recognize/reward status - Communicate special values - Promotion - Maximize share of customer

High Purchase Amount/Infrequent

A bad experience often keeps customers from returning to
the same brand in this category. Think about automobiles.
When customers are contemplating another purchase, they
often think about the experience they had during and after
they made their last purchase. It's important for you to
reinforce all the positive reasons why the customer selected
your brand in the past. It's also important to gauge
customer satisfaction and do things to improve it. Owning
up to a problem and fixing it can earn your brand a great
deal of respect from a customer. Promotional currency
programs aren't usually the way to go here. It's contact
strategy.

High Purchase Amount/Frequent

Both promotional currency and contact strategy work in this category. Look hard at soft benefits, too. The choice may come down to whether or not you have much direct competition. If competition is intense and if many of the competitors look similar, you may need promotional currency to break the tie.

Low Purchase Amount/Infrequent

This is not really an appropriate category for any of the approaches to loyalty that I've illustrated. An infrequent purchase of a low purchase amount doesn't usually support loyalty tactics. The economics just don't work. Examination of this quadrant means taking a closer look at the transaction size. Toothpicks, baking soda and ketchup: forget about it, unless they are teamed up with other products (consumer packaged goods companies may combine multiple brands for a powerful program). For products in the $40 to $99 range, consider some of the strategies I've outlined for high purchase amount/infrequent.

Low Purchase Amount/Frequent

This category also supports both promotional currency and contact strategy. Other hard benefits programs such as fee-based discount programs can work (although I'm not a big fan of programs based solely on a discount). These tend to be more promotionally oriented categories of business and very competitive. Some programs look like a combination of loyalty and promotion (look at McDonald's Road2Rewards).

The Nature of Defection

Let's examine how customers defect. To facilitate this examination, let's organize business types into three categories:

- Repetitive transaction businesses
- Subscription businesses
- Big ticket/infrequent

Repetitive Transaction Businesses

These fall into the two "frequent" quadrants in the velocity and size model. These are things that customers purchase on a fairly regular basis. Retail, e-tail, travel, dining, video rental and more. Every time a customer walks out the door or leaves your website, you have no idea if they're ever coming back. This is what I call passive defection.

Subscription Businesses

Products and services that customers subscribe to. In this category, customers must take action to terminate a relationship. They must "fire" your brand. This is what I call active defection. Products in this category include telecommunications services, Internet service providers, utilities and cable television.

Big Ticket/Infrequent

These are items that fall into the upper left quadrant
of the velocity and size model. It includes thing
such as vacations, vehicles, houses and appliances.
Defection here is passive. Customers don't need to
tell you they're not coming back.

The Nature of Strategy

Here's how customers defect:

Repetitive transaction businesses	Passive defection
Subscription businesses	Active defection
Big ticket/infrequent	Passive defection

Here's what to do about it. Some potential approaches.
There is some overlap and interaction between these
suggestions and those I've laid out under the velocity and
size model. You'll need to put it all together and consider
your own unique business conditions to make your choice.

Repetitive Transaction Approach

Promotional currency or contact strategy. If you use
promotional currency, look hard at automatic redemption
and expiration dates. Be sure to use the redemption process
as a way to increase transaction velocity and sales. The key
here is to drive repeat transactions and build a pattern of
customer behavior.

Subscription Businesses Approach

Promotional currency works here, but look at potentially implementing a vesting period. Make sure customers have a reason to stay with your brand for a period of time before they can redeem for something. Communication and education may also be effective. I provided an example earlier of a telecommunications company (a subscription business) using communication to educate customers. Look at soft benefits also. The key here is to take customers out of the market. Give them a reason to ignore competitive offers. The promotional currency model with vesting period does this particularly well.

Big Ticket/Infrequent Approach

Remind customers why they bought your brand before. Gauge customer satisfaction and do something to fix problems. Anticipate when customers are considering another purchase in the category. Engage the customer in a dialog and encourage them to tell you when they're back in the market. The key here is to influence the likelihood the customer will buy your brand again. Timing is very important.

Integration of Channels, Products and Brands

We're sometimes our own worst enemy. We confuse customers with our artificial barriers and silos that keep our channels, products and brands from communicating with one consistent voice.

When considering loyalty, work hard to bring together all of the manifestations of your brand that the customer sees. Bring together your off-line and on-line businesses. Bring together products and brands.

Look at what Barnes & Noble has done. The Readers' Advantage program brings together its traditional retail business with its on-line business (even though they are different organizations). I commend them for this.

Look at what Musicland has done. They have united four different retail brands under one umbrella program. Kudos to them.

Bank of Asia is particularly impressive. Banks have many product silos that confuse customers. Bank of Asia has integrated debit cards, credit cards, deposit accounts, loans, ATM usage and money transfer under one program. Outstanding.

Loyalty strategy requires a high level of commitment. Unifying channels, products and brands require decisive and persuasive leadership.

Chapter Ten

Measurement

Back in the second chapter of this book, I used the example of a fictitious retailer known as Duffy's Depot to illustrate lifetime value. Now we're going to get into some of the nuts and bolts of measurement, continuing to use the Duffy's Depot example.

This is not a book about measurement. I'm going to review enough about measurement to get you started. If you have some analytical training or experience you may not need much more than what I'm going to share with you. If you're an experienced analyst in the world of direct marketing you may find my examples to be fundamental.

Lifetime Value as Measurement

Lifetime value itself is not a measure of success. But changes in lifetime value can be a measure of success. The dilemma is this. Lifetime value is a long-term concept. Remember the example we used before? We were looking five years into the future and discounting expected cash flows to present value. It's an important concept to review with others in your company, but the fundamental reality of today's business climate is that often programs must pay for themselves rather quickly. We need to look at ROI.

Control Groups

Before getting into ROI, we must have a quick review of control groups. If you know what a control group is, skip this. Otherwise, read on.

A control group is used to isolate the impact of a marketing program or group of marketing programs. A control group is a random group of like customers held out of the marketing program. Behavior of customers in the control group is compared to the behavior of the customers in the marketing program. Generally all other things are considered to be equal, so the differences in behavior between the two groups are considered to be attributable to the program.

Here's a simple example. Let's say we're executing a direct mail program within our contact strategy. We select customers in the highest spending segment because we're going to send a special recognition mailing. There are 100,000 customers in the segment. Before executing the mailing, we randomly extract 10,000 of those customers to be our control group (groups much smaller than 10,000 can raise issues about statistical validity). The control group customers are similar in make up to those who will receive the mailing.

Let's say we analyze spending behavior during a period of time following the mailing. I can't tell you absolutely how long a period of time you should analyze. You should look at response levels each week after the mailing occurs and determine the point at which there no longer appears to be a difference between customers in the mail group and those in the control group (there are more rigorous statistical techniques for getting precise about this). Suppose we conclude that the effectiveness of the mailing ended after four weeks, and the total spending in the two groups is as follows:

Spending

	Spending
Mail group	$ 135,000
Control group	$ 11,500

We want to determine how much incremental spending occurred. To do so, we first must adjust these numbers. We must project what the control group spending would have been if it were the same size as the mail group. Remember that we had 100,000 customers to start with. We held 10,000 out as our control group so 90,000 received the mailing. In this case I simply multiply the control group sales by nine to make it an apples to apples comparison with the mail group.

Here are the adjusted numbers:

	Spending
Mail group	$ 135,000
Control group	$ 103,500
Incremental	$ 31,500

That's the concept of a control group and how it's used.

Return on Investment (ROI)

Let's first take a look at calculating ROI on a contact strategy. We've been through the control group explanation so that gives us a nice head start. With a contact strategy it's best to hold out a control group for the entire period you're testing the contact strategy (six months to a year). It's best to have a control group from each segment or, if you select one control group, at least examine it to ensure that it represents each of your segments proportionately. For instance, if a particular segment represents about seven percent of your customer base, it should represent about seven percent of the control group.

Once you've completed your test period, calculate the incremental spending as we did in our control group explanation. Convert incremental spending into incremental gross profit (or incremental contribution margin, if that's an approach more commonly used in your company). We're trying to determine the portion of incremental spending that goes to cover fixed costs and profit. Let's assume we're going to use gross profit and it's at a rate of 35%.

The next component we'll need to calculate ROI is the amount we invested to make the results happen. It's the budget we applied toward our segmentation and contact strategy to generate the incremental gross profit.

Let's assume the following:

Incremental Sales	$ 1,000,000
Incremental Gross Profit	$ 350,000
Budget Spent	$ 250,000
ROI	40%

The ROI is calculated as (Incremental gross profit – Budget spent)/Budget spent. This tells us that we put $250,000 into the segmentation and contact strategy. That's the budget we spent. It's the investment component of return on investment. We generated $350,000 in incremental gross profit. That paid for our $250,000 investment with $100,000 to spare. The $100,000 is 40% of the $250,000. That's ROI.

Promotional Currency ROI

Before jumping into an ROI calculation, we must consider some of the promotional currency idiosyncrasies. Let's assume we have a program at Duffy's Depot in which members earn five points per dollar spent. Once a member earns 500 points, a five dollar reward is issued. This looks like a program funded at a rate of five percent.

This apparent five percent funding rate is what I call a gross funding rate. To calculate our real cost, we must convert the gross funding rate (GFR) to a net funding rate (NFR).

The first thing we must adjust for is breakage. Breakage is the currency never redeemed. Over time you'll get a sense of what the breakage will be in your program. Breakage typically ranges from 20% to 60%. For our calculations, let's settle on 40% breakage. If 40% of our currency is not redeemed, 60% is redeemed.

The second thing we must adjust for is cost of goods sold. This assumes we're giving away our own product as a reward. (If that's not the case, you'll need to adjust based on the actual cost of the rewards you're giving away.) Cost of goods sold is (1 – gross profit). We've been using a gross profit of 35%. So our cost of goods sold is 65%. When we sell something for one dollar, our cost is $.65.

The NFR = GFR * percent of currency redeemed * cost of goods sold.

Using this example, NFR = 5% * 60% * 65%.

NFR = 1.95%. That's the funding rate after adjusting for actual redemption and cost of goods sold.

Let's walk through an ROI scenario with our NFR. We're still using the same program scenario for Duffy's Depot. Here are some additional assumptions and a calculation of ROI.

- NFR of 1.95%
- Communication cost of $1.50 per member, per year
  (assumes we're using e-mail effectively)
- Infrastructure cost of $500,000
- 500,000 members
- Sales lift of 15%

Annual Program Sales	$	575,000,000
Portion of Sales that is Incremental	$	75,000,000
Incremental Gross Margin	$	26,250,000
Funding (1.95% of sales)	$	11,212,500
Communication	$	750,000
Infrastructure	$	500,000
Total Program Costs	$	12,462,500
ROI		111%

If you're interested in calculating the breakeven point,
simply adjust the incremental sales number until the ROI
becomes 0.

Here's what the breakeven numbers look like:

Annual Program Sales	$	533,284,000
Portion of Sales that is Incremental	$	33,284,000
Incremental Gross Margin	$	11,649,400
Funding (1.95% of sales)	$	10,399,038
Communication	$	750,000
Infrastructure	$	500,000
Total Program Costs	$	11,649,038
ROI		0.00%
Breakeven Incremental Sales Lift		6.66%

In this scenario it requires a 6.66% lift in sales to breakeven.

Research for Measurement and Insight

Everything we've looked at so far is linked to changes in behavior. We should not overlook changes in customer attitude. Behavior is a clear indication of what's happening now. Attitude is an indication of what's likely to happen in the future.

If you have been able to maintain a control group, you can conduct sample research on customers in your program versus those in your control group. If you have not been able to maintain a control group, you can conduct sample research on those customers in your program versus those who are not. This second method has some obvious flaws in terms of bias. But it's better than nothing.

Qualitative research is good for getting directional insight into your program and feedback from customers. Quantitative research can uncover signs that your program has impact beyond just what you can ascertain from behavior measurement.

The following are some things to look for in your research. In each point I'm referring to differences between customers in the program versus the control group, or between customers in the program versus not in the program.

- What brand do members mention first in your category?
- When prompted with a list of choices in your category and asked to rank order the choices, where do members place your brand?
- How do members rate your quality, value, price, service, selection and convenience versus your competition?
- How likely are members to complain rather than quietly defect?
- How likely are members to refer friends and relatives to your brand?

This is a start. If you have a regular tracking study you do with customers I suggest segmenting it based on membership (members versus control group or members versus non-members). Sample research is an important way to augment your behavior measurement. It provides additional texture about what your loyalty efforts do for your brand.

Chapter Eleven

Evolution And
Exit Strategy

Evolution

The pursuit of loyalty is never complete. The process of getting and keeping your house in order is ongoing. The process of cultivating loyalty through tactical programs is perpetual as well. But you can't let your efforts become stale. You must keep changing and refining your program. Things must remain fresh through the eyes of the customer.

Keep your communication relevant. Introduce new features and benefits, but maintain the consistency of your program brand. Earlier in this book I discussed the potential of an advisory board of customers. That's a good way to ensure your program evolution is customer-focused.

Think about re-launching your program each year. It gives you a reason to ensure that it doesn't get neglected and drift into obscurity.

Exit Strategy

Think about this before you launch a defined program. It's not really an issue with a contact strategy.

Defined programs have rules. Some times these rules are called terms and conditions. Be sure to include appropriate language in your terms and conditions that allows you to end the program at any time. Look at written terms and conditions from a variety of programs in the marketplace to get some guidance on what to include.

Reasons for Ending a Program

There are a variety of reasons why programs end:

- The program is not deemed to be successful. You've determined that the program has not created acceptable business results. If this is the case, the program is probably not very popular with customers.
- The program is too popular, but not successful. Customers love the program, but it does not create incremental profit. This may happen if the economic conditions of your business change after you launch the program. I saw this happen with a video-rental chain in the early 1990's. They launched a program with a funding rate tied to number of rentals (rather than dollars spent). Their rewards were third-party merchandise. The price of a video rental dropped by 50% as a result of price wars. Their program costs

remained fixed but their revenue was cut in half. This situation requires a little more finesse. You'll get many phone calls from customers when you announce the end. Be prepared.

- Internal reasons. Frankly, some times this happens when management changes in an organization. New leaders want to disassociate themselves with the marketing programs introduced by previous management.

Checklist for Ending a Program

You must let members know well in advance. I suggest at least 90 days before the end of the program. Be honest. Let members know why the program is ending. Do so as plainly as possible.

If you have a customer service operation, be sure your agents are well prepared for the calls they'll receive. Stage the mailing of customer notifications so the phones don't ring off the hook all at once. Prepare statements for the media. It's better to be over prepared.

Develop a plan for how you'll settle accounts with customers. If this is a promotional currency program, let customers know the last date through which they'll earn currency. Develop a policy for the final settlement. You may want to consider rounding up balances that are within 20% of a redemption level. Be generous. You're pulling something out from under your customers.

If your program requires an annual fee you'll need to refund a portion or all of it. Determine when and how you'll settle the fees.

One way to anticipate your exit strategy is to announce
your program with an end date from the very start. You
can always announce good news to members when you
decide to renew it for another year.

Chapter Twelve

Do Something

That's what I label the last chapter of this book. Do something. The help and guidance that I've presented in this book is intended to help companies take action. Positive action to build customer loyalty and increase revenue.

Building customer loyalty is an important business strategy. It requires honest assessment, sound planning and well-executed marketing tactics. The results are measured in retention rates and share of customer. The bottom line is long-term business growth.

I urge you to avoid the paralysis that affects too many businesses and too many business leaders. Don't get me wrong, I'm not advocating maverick, shoot-from-the-hip style marketing. I'm advocating courage. The courage to lead your business by example toward stronger customer relationships. The courage to innovate. The courage to admit imperfection and to confront mediocrity.

Remember my opening line from Chapter Four. "I just work here." That's the mediocrity I urge you to confront and overcome. Get your house in order. Assess your situation openly and honestly with the Customer Loyalty Audit. Use the examples, principles and approaches in this book to keep customers longer and earn more of each customer's business. Do it now. Before your competitor does.

Trademark Acknowledgements

The following names are trademarks of their respective owners:

AAdvantage
Adolpus Hotel
Advance Auto Parts
Advantage Checking
Amazon.com
America West
American Airlines
AT&T
Bank Champaign
Bank of America
Bank of Asia
Barnes & Noble
Blockbuster Rewards
Blockbuster Video
BN.COM
Book Magazine
Borders
Brentano's
China Airlines
Coca-Cola
Delta Airlines
Dillards
Dividend Miles
Evian
Extra Value Meal
ExxonMobil
Free Flix
Gap
General Motors
Hawaiian Airlines
Home Depot
Imation
Korean Air

Lowe's
Macy's
McDonald's
MCI Worldcom
MCI Worldcom
Midwest Express
Old Navy
Platinum Visa Card With Rewards
Preferred Reader
Prime Rewards
RadioShack
Readers' Advantage
Rewards Imation Program
Ritz-Carlton
Road2Rewards
Saks Fifth Avenue
Southwest Airlines
Sprint
The Repair Shop at RadioShack
The Right Start
The Sharper Image
Toys R Us
United Airlines
Upgrade to Evian
uPromise
US Airways
Visa
Waldenbooks
Walden-By-Mail
Wells Fargo
Wells Fargo Rewards
Wendy's